THE YALE SHAKESPEARE

Revised Edition

———————————

General Editors

Helge Kökeritz and Charles T. Prouty

———————————

Published on the fund

given to the Yale University Press in 191?

by the members of the

Kingsley Trust Association

(Scroll and Key Society of Yale College)

to commemorate the seventy-fifth anniversary

of the founding of the society

THE YALE SHAKESPEARE

THE TRAGEDY OF

KING RICHARD THE SECOND

Edited by Robert T. Petersson

NEW HAVEN AND LONDON:

YALE UNIVERSITY PRESS

© *1921, 1957 by Yale University Press, Inc.*

FIRST PUBLISHED   MAY 1921
REVISED EDITION   NOVEMBER 1957
FOURTH PRINTING   MARCH 1965

Printed in the United States of America

*Published on the fund given
to the Yale University Press in 1917
by the members of the
Kingsley Trust Association
(Scroll and Key Society of Yale College)
to commemorate the seventy-fifth anniversary
of the founding of the society*

Preface of the General Editors

AS the late Professor Tucker Brooke has observed, practically all modern editions of Shakespeare are 18th-century versions of the plays, based on the additions, alterations, and emendations of editors of that period. It has been our purpose, as it was Professor Brooke's, to give the modern reader Shakespeare's plays in the approximate form of their original appearance.

About half the plays appeared in quarto form before the publication of the First Folio in 1623. Thus for a large number of plays the only available text is that of the Folio. In the case of quarto plays our policy has been to use that text as the basis of the edition, unless it is clear that the text has been contaminated.

Interesting for us today is the fact that there are no act or scene divisions in the Quartos with the exception of *Othello*, which does mark Acts I, II, IV, and V but lacks indications of scenes. Even in the Folio, although act divisions are generally noted, only a part of the scenes are divided. In no case, either in Quarto or Folio, is there any indication of the place of action. The manifold scene divisions for the battle in such a play as *Antony and Cleopatra*, together with such locations as "Another part of the field," are the additions of the 18th century.

We have eliminated all indications of the place and time of action, because there is no authority for them in the originals and because Shakespeare gives such information, when it is requisite for understanding the play, through the dialogue of the actors. We have been sparing in our use of added scene and, in some

v

cases, act divisions, because these frequently impede the flow of the action, which in Shakespeare's time was curiously like that of modern films.

Spelling has been modernized except when the original clearly indicates a pronunciation unlike our own, e.g. *desart* (desert), *divel* (devil), *banket* (banquet), and often in such Elizabethan syncopations as *stolne* (stol'n), and *tane* (ta'en). In reproducing such forms we have followed the inconsistent usage of the original.

We have also preserved the original capitalization when this is a part of the meaning. In like manner we have tended to adopt the lineation of the original in many cases where modern editors print prose as verse or verse as prose. We have, moreover, followed the original punctuation wherever it was practicable.

In verse we print a final *-ed* to indicate its full syllabic value, otherwise *'d*. In prose we have followed the inconsistencies of the original in this respect.

Our general practice has been to include in footnotes all information a reader needs for immediate understanding of the given page. In somewhat empiric fashion we repeat glosses as we think the reader needs to be reminded of the meaning. Further information is given in notes (indicated by the letter *N* in the footnotes) to be found at the back of each volume. Appendices deal with the text and sources of the play.

Square brackets indicate material not found in the original text. Long emendations or lines taken from another authoritative text of a play are indicated in the footnotes for the information of the reader. We have silently corrected obvious typographical errors.

CONTENTS

[THE ACTORS' NAMES

KING RICHARD THE SECOND
JOHN OF GAUNT, *Duke of Lancaster* ⎱ *uncles of the king*
EDMUND OF LANGLEY, *Duke of York* ⎰
HENRY, *surnamed* BOLINGBROKE, *Duke of Hereford, son to John of Gaunt; afterward* KING HENRY IV
DUKE OF AUMERLE, *son to the Duke of York*
THOMAS MOWBRAY, *Duke of Norfolk*
DUKE OF SURREY
EARL OF SALISBURY
LORD BERKELEY
BUSHY ⎱
BAGOT ⎰ *servants to King Richard*
GREEN
EARL OF NORTHUMBERLAND
HENRY PERCY, *surnamed* HOTSPUR, **his son**
LORD ROSS
LORD WILLOUGHBY
LORD FITZWATER
BISHOP OF CARLISLE
ABBOT OF WESTMINSTER
LORD MARSHAL
SIR STEPHEN SCROOP
SIR PIERCE OF EXTON
Captain of a band of Welshmen

QUEEN *to King Richard*
DUCHESS OF YORK
DUCHESS OF GLOUCESTER
Lady attending on the queen

Lords, heralds, officers, soldiers, two gardeners, Keeper, Messenger, Groom, and other attendants

SCENE: *England and Wales*]

The Actors' . . . Wales N. (N refers throughout to the corresponding note given at the end of the text.)

THE TRAGEDY OF KING RICHARD
THE SECOND
Act I

SCENE 1

Enter King Richard, John of Gaunt, with other nobles and attendants.

King Richard. Old John of Gaunt, time-honor'd Lancaster,
Hast thou, according to thy oath and band,
Brought hither Henry Herford, thy bold son,
Here to make good the boist'rous late appeal—
Which then our leisure would not let me hear—
Against the Duke of Norfolk, Thomas Mowbray?
Gaunt. I have, my liege.
King Richard. Tell me, moreover, hast thou sounded him,
If he appeal the duke on ancient malice,
Or worthily, as a good subject should,   10
On some known ground of treachery in him?

Act I, Scene 1 N. SD King Richard N. (SD is used throughout to indicate stage direction.) 1 John of Gaunt N. 2 band bond. 3 Herford disyllabic (read 'her-' or 'har-') N. 4 late six weeks previously. appeal accusation or challenge. 9 appeal accuse. on ancient malice because of long-standing enmity.

Gaunt. As near as I could sift him on that
　argument,
On some apparent danger seen in him
Aim'd at your highness, no inveterate malice.
　King Richard. Then call them to our presence.
　Face to face,　　　　　　　　　　　　　　15
And frowning brow to brow, ourselves will hear
The accuser and the accused freely speak.
High-stomach'd are they both, and full of ire,
In rage deaf as the sea, hasty as fire.

Enter Bullingbrooke and Mowbray.

Bullingbrooke. Many years of happy days befall
My gracious sovereign, my most loving liege!　21
　Mowbray. Each day still better other's happiness,
Until the heavens, envying earth's good hap,
Add an immortal title to your crown!
　King Richard. We thank you both. Yet one but
　flatters us,　　　　　　　　　　　　　　25
As well appeareth by the cause you come;
Namely, to appeal each other of high treason.
Cousin of Herford, what dost thou object
Against the Duke of Norfolk, Thomas Mowbray?
　Bullingbrooke. First—heaven be the record to my
　speech!—　　　　　　　　　　　　　　30
In the devotion of a subject's love,

12 As near . . . argument N. **sift** examine. **argument** subject.
14 **inveterate** trisyllabic. 17 **The accuser and the accused** read
'th' accuser and th' accuséd.' 18 **High-stomach'd** haughty. 20
Bullingbrooke Henry Bolingbroke, Duke of Hereford (see I.1.3 N)
N. **Many . . . befall** N. 22 **better other's** make better the previous day's. 23 **heavens** monosyllabic. **envying** stressed — $\acute{-}$ —
(rhymes with 'replying'). 24 **Add . . . crown** add immortality
to kingship. 27 **to appeal** read 't' appeal.'
　　2

Tend'ring the precious safety of my prince
And free from other misbegotten hate,
Come I appellant to this princely presence.
Now, Thomas Mowbray, do I turn to thee,   35
And mark my greeting well, for what I speak
My body shall make good upon this earth,
Or my divine soul answer it in heaven.
Thou art a traitor and a miscreant,
Too good to be so, and too bad to live,   40
Since the more fair and crystal is the sky,
The uglier seem the clouds that in it fly.
Once more, the more to aggravate the note,
With a foul traitor's name stuff I thy throat
And wish—so please my sovereign—ere I move,   45
What my tongue speaks, my right-drawn sword may
    prove.
  Mowbray. Let not my cold words here accuse my
    zeal.
'Tis not the trial of a woman's war,
The bitter clamor of two eager tongues,
Can arbitrate this cause betwixt us twain.   50
The blood is hot that must be cool'd for this.
Yet can I not of such tame patience boast
As to be hush'd and naught at all to say.
First, the fair reverence of your highness curbs me
From giving reins and spurs to my free speech,   55
Which else would post until it had return'd

32 Tend'ring caring dearly for. 34 appellant N. 40 good i.e. high
in rank. 43 aggravate the note increase the insult. note brand or
stigma of disgrace (from Latin *nota*). 46 right-drawn drawn in a
rightful cause. 47 accuse cast doubt upon. 49 eager sharp, biting
(from French *aigre*). 51 cool'd i.e. by death. 54 reverence of
respect for. 56 post speed.

These terms of treason doubled down his throat.
Setting aside his high blood's royalty,
And let him be no kinsman to my liege,
I do defy him, and I spit at him,   60
Call him a slanderous coward and a villain;
Which to maintain I would allow him odds
And meet him, were I tied to run afoot
Even to the frozen ridges of the Alps,
Or any other ground inhabitable,   65
Where ever Englishman durst set his foot.
Meantime let this defend my loyalty—
By all my hopes most falsely doth he lie.
    Bullingbrooke. Pale trembling coward, there I
        throw my gage,
Disclaiming here the kinred of the king,   70
And lay aside my high blood's royalty,
Which fear, not reverence, makes thee to except.
If guilty dread have left thee so much strength
As to take up mine honor's pawn, then stoop.
By that, and all the rites of knighthood else,   75
Will I make good against thee, arm to arm,
What I have spoke, or thou canst worse devise.

---

57 These terms of treason i.e. *traitor* and *miscreant* (l. 39).
doubled F *doubly.* (F refers throughout to the First Folio of
1623, F2 to the Second Folio, etc.) **58 royalty** Bolingbroke was
the king's first cousin. **59 let him be** assuming that he is. **63 tied**
obliged, bound N. **64 Even** read 'e'en' (as elsewhere). **65 inhabitable** uninhabitable. **67 this** i.e. the statement in l. 68. **68
hopes** i.e. hopes of salvation. **69 gage** pledge (probably his iron
glove or gauntlet). **70 Disclaiming** renouncing. **kinred** old form of
'kindred.' **the king** other Qq, F *a King.* **72 to except** take exception to, protest against. **74 pawn** the gage (l. 69). **75 rites** F2
rights. **else** besides this. **77 thou . . . devise** N.

Mowbray. I take it up, and by that sword I swear
Which gently laid my knighthood on my shoulder,
I'll answer thee in any fair degree   80
Or chivalrous design of knightly trial;
And when I mount, alive may I not light,
If I be traitor or unjustly fight!

  King Richard. What doth our cousin lay to Mow-
          bray's charge?
It must be great that can inherit us   85
So much as of a thought of ill in him.

  Bullingbrooke. Look, what I speak, my life shall
          prove it true:
That Mowbray hath receiv'd eight thousand nobles
In name of lendings for your highness' soldiers,
The which he hath detain'd for lewd employments,
Like a false traitor and injurious villain.   91
Besides I say, and will in battle prove,
Or here or elsewhere to the furthest verge
That ever was survey'd by English eye,
That all the treasons for these eighteen years   95
Complotted and contrived in this land
Fetch from false Mowbray their first head and
          spring.
Further I say, and further will maintain
Upon his bad life to make all this good,
That he did plot the Duke of Gloucester's death,

80 **in any fair degree** to any extent compatible with chivalric code.
82 **light** alight. 85–6 **inherit . . . thought** make us have as
much as a thought. 89 **lendings** money advanced in lieu of
regular pay. 90 **lewd** base, mean. 91 **injurious** pernicious. 93 **Or
here or** either here or. **verge** boundary. 95 **these eighteen years**
i.e. since Wat Tyler's insurrection in 1381. 97 **Fetch** derive;
other Qq *Fetcht*; F *Fetch'd*. 98 **maintain** undertake. 100 **Duke of
Gloucester's death** N.

5

Suggest his soon-believing adversaries,   101
And consequently, like a traitor coward,
Sluic'd out his innocent soul through streams of
    blood,
Which blood, like sacrificing Abel's, cries,
Even from the tongueless caverns of the earth,   105
To me for justice and rough chastisement.
And by the glorious worth of my descent,
This arm shall do it, or this life be spent.
   King Richard. How high a pitch his resolution
    soars!   109
Thomas of Norfolk, what say'st thou to this?
   Mowbray. O, let my sovereign turn away his face,
And bid his ears a little while be deaf,
Till I have told this slander of his blood
How God and good men hate so foul a liar!
   King Richard. Mowbray, impartial are our eyes
    and ears.   115
Were he my brother, nay, my kingdom's heir,
As he is but my father's brother's son,
Now, by my scepter's awe, I make a vow,
Such neighbor nearness to our sacred blood
Should nothing privilege him, nor partialize   120
The unstooping firmness of my upright soul.

101–3 Suggest . . . blood N. 101 Suggest . . . adversaries did
secretly incite his credulous enemies against him. 102 consequently subsequently. 106 me as Gaunt's eldest son and Gloucester's nephew. 107 worth honor. 108 or perhaps meaning 'before'
(see I.1.77 N). 109 pitch high point of a falcon's flight (a term
in falconry). 113 this slander . . . blood i.e. this man (Hereford) who is a disgrace to his ancestry. 116 my kingdom's *Four
kingdomes.* 118 my F; not in Qq. my scepter's awe by the honor
due my scepter. 119 neighbor nearness N. sacred blood N. 120
nothing not at all. partialize make partial.

He is our subject, Mowbray, so art thou.
Free speech and fearless I to thee allow.
   Mowbray. Then, Bullingbrooke, as low as to thy
     heart,   124
Through the false passage of thy throat, thou liest!
Three parts of that receipt I had for Callice
Disburs'd I duly to his highness' soldiers.
The other part reserv'd I by consent,
For that my sovereign liege was in my debt
Upon remainder of a dear account   130
Since last I went to France to fetch his queen.
Now swallow down that lie! For Gloucester's death,
I slew him not, but to my own disgrace
Neglected my sworn duty in that case.
For you, my noble Lord of Lancaster,   135
The honorable father to my foe,
Once did I lay an ambush for your life—
A trespass that doth vex my grieved soul.
But ere I last receiv'd the sacrament
I did confess it, and exactly begg'd   140
Your grace's pardon, and I hope I had it.
This is my fault. As for the rest appeal'd,
It issues from the rancor of a villain,

---

124 **as low . . . heart** from the bottom of your base heart.
126 **that receipt . . . Callice** the money received from the
Calais garrison. **Callice** Calais (pronounced 'Cal'iss.') 129 **For**
that because (as frequently). 130 **Upon remainder . . . account**
as part balance of a heavy debt you owe me. 131 **last** lately.
queen N. 132 **For** as for (also in l. 135). 135–41 **For you . . . it**
N. 139 **But** Q (Huth), F; Q (Devonshire, Capell, Petworth), Q2,
Q3 *Ah but;* Q4, Q5 *Ah, but.* (Q refers throughout to the First
Quarto of 1597. Q2 to the Second Quarto, etc.) 140 **exactly** ex-
plicitly.

A recreant and most degenerate traitor;
Which in myself I boldly will defend,   145
And interchangeably hurl down my gage
Upon this overweening traitor's foot,
To prove myself a loyal gentleman
Even in the best blood chamber'd in his bosom.
In haste whereof, most heartily I pray   150
Your highness to assign our trial day.
  King Richard. Wrath-kindled gentleman, be rul'd
          by me;
Let's purge this choler without letting blood.
This we prescribe, though no physician;
Deep malice makes too deep incision.   155
Forget, forgive, conclude and be agreed;
Our doctors say this is no month to bleed.
Good uncle, let this end where it begun;
We'll calm the Duke of Norfolk, you your son.   159
  Gaunt. To be a make-peace shall become my age.
Throw down, my son, the Duke of Norfolk's gage.
  King Richard. And, Norfolk, throw down his.
  Gaunt.   When,
          Harry? When?
Obedience bids I should not bid again.
  King Richard. Norfolk, throw down, we bid. There
          is no boot.

144 **recreant** one false to his faith (or perhaps an adjective).
degenerate (trisyllabic) degenerated from his race or blood.
145 **Which** i.e. the assertion of l. 144. **in myself** in my own person.
146 **interchangeably** in exchange for Bolingbroke's challenge.
150 **In haste whereof** to hasten which proof. 152 **gentleman** F
Gentlemen. 153 **choler** anger N. 154 **physician** four syllables (like
incision in the next line). 156 **conclude** come to terms. 157 **no**
month to bleed N. 158 **begun** began. 163 **Obedience bids** Qq, F
mistakenly print the words twice in ll. 163–4. 164 **no boot** no
help, i.e. no use resisting.

8

Mowbray. Myself I throw, dread sovereign, at thy
  foot.   165
My life thou shalt command but not my shame.
The one my duty owes, but my fair name,
Despite of death that lives upon my grave,
To dark dishonor's use thou shalt not have.
I am disgrac'd, impeach'd, and baffled here;   170
Pierc'd to the soul with Slander's venom'd spear,
The which no balm can cure but his heart-blood
Which breath'd this poison.

King Richard.   Rage must be with-
  stood.
Give me his gage; lions make leopards tame.

Mowbray. Yea, but not change his spots. Take
  but my shame,   175
And I resign my gage. My dear lord,
The purest treasure mortal times afford
Is spotless reputation. That away,
Men are but gilded loam or painted clay.
A jewel in a ten-times-barr'd-up chest   180
Is a bold spirit in a loyal breast.
Mine honor is my life, both grow in one;
Take honor from me and my life is done.
Then, dear my liege, mine honor let me try.
In that I live, and for that will I die.   185

King Richard. Cousin, throw up your gage. Do
  you begin.

168 that antecedent: *name* (l. 167). 170 impeach'd accused.
baffled utterly dishonored. 173 Which who (antecedent: *his*,
meaning 'of him'). breath'd uttered. 174 lions . . . leopards N.
175 change his spots see Jeremiah 13:23 (which Mowbray has
in mind). 176 gage. My dear N. 177 mortal times earthly life.
184 try test by combat. 186 throw up surrender the gage, give
up the challenge; Qq; F *throw downe* N.

Bullingbrooke. O, God defend my soul from such
    deep sin!
Shall I seem crestfallen in my father's sight?
Or with pale beggar-fear impeach my height
Before this outdar'd dastard? Ere my tongue   190
Shall wound my honor with such feeble wrong,
Or sound so base a parle, my teeth shall tear
The slavish motive of recanting fear
And spit it bleeding in his high disgrace,   194
Where shame doth harbor, even in Mowbray's face.
                                                    [*Exit Gaunt.*]
King Richard. We were not born to sue, but to
    command,
Which since we cannot do to make you friends,
Be ready, as your lives shall answer it,
At Coventry upon Saint Lambert's day.
There shall your swords and lances arbitrate   200
The swelling difference of your settled hate.
Since we cannot atone you, we shall see
Justice design the victor's chivalry.
Lord Marshal, command our officers at arms   204
Be ready to direct these home alarms.   [*Exeunt.*]

---

187 God Qq; F *heauen* N. deep Qq; F *foule.* 189 beggar-fear fear
befitting a miserable beggar; Q, F; other Qq *beggr-face.* impeach
my height call in question my high name and rank. 191 feeble
wrong i.e. of speaking in so weak and craven a tone. 192 sound
. . . parle N. 193 motive instrument, i.e. the tongue. 194 his
its (or possibly Mowbray's). SD Exit Gaunt N. 199 Saint Lambert's day September 17, celebrating the early 8th-century
martyr. 201 of resulting from. 202 atone reconcile (make 'at one').
we shall Q; other Qq, F *you shall.* 203 design . . . chivalry
designate the knight whose prowess will prevail. 204 Marshal N.
205 home alarms civil conflicts (in contrast to the Irish rebellion
perhaps hinted at here).

10

SCENE 2

Enter John of Gaunt with the Duchess of Gloucester.

Gaunt. Alas, the part I had in Woodstock's blood
Doth more solicit me than your exclaims
To stir against the butchers of his life!
But since correction lieth in those hands
Which made the fault that we cannot correct,   5
Put we our quarrel to the will of heaven,
Who, when they see the hours ripe on earth,
Will rain hot vengeance on offenders' heads.
    Duchess. Finds brotherhood in thee no sharper
        spur?
Hath love in thy old blood no living fire?   10
Edward's seven sons, whereof thyself art one,
Were as seven vials of his sacred blood,
Or seven fair branches springing from one root.
Some of those seven are dried by nature's course,
Some of those branches by the Destinies cut;   15
But Thomas, my dear lord, my life, my Gloucester,
One vial full of Edward's sacred blood,
One flourishing branch of his most royal root,
Is crack'd, and all the precious liquor spilt,

1 the part . . . blood my fraternal relationship to Woodstock.
Woodstock's of Thomas of Woodstock, late Duke of Gloucester;
F *Glousters*. blood N. 2 solicit rouse. 4 those hands i.e. Richard's.
6 Put . . . to let us entrust our cause to. heaven i.e. heavenly
powers (frequently a plural in Shakespeare). 7 they i.e. heaven
(l. 6). 11 Edward's seven sons N. 14–21 Some . . . ax N. 14
Some . . . dried some of the seven vials are empty, i.e. some
of the sons are dead.

Is hack'd down, and his summer leaves all faded, 20
By Envy's hand and Murder's bloody ax.
Ah, Gaunt, his blood was thine! That bed, that
    womb,
That metal, that self-mold that fashioned thee
Made him a man; and though thou liv'st and
    breath'st,
Yet art thou slain in him. Thou dost consent 25
In some large measure to thy father's death
In that thou seest thy wretched brother die,
Who was the model of thy father's life.
Call it not patience, Gaunt; it is despair.
In suff'ring thus thy brother to be slaught'red, 30
Thou show'st the naked pathway to thy life,
Teaching stern Murder how to butcher thee.
That which in mean men we entitle patience
Is pale cold cowardice in noble breasts.
What shall I say? To safeguard thine own life, 35
The best way is to venge my Gloucester's death.
  Gaunt. God's is the quarrel; for God's substitute,
His deputy anointed in His sight,
Hath caus'd his death; the which if wrongfully,
Let heaven revenge; for I may never lift 40
An angry arm against His minister.
  Duchess. Where then, alas, may I complain myself?
  Gaunt. To God, the widow's champion and defense.

21 **Envy's hand** i.e. the hand of malice. 23 **self-mold** selfsame
mold. 29 **patience** self-control. 30 **suff'ring** enduring. **slaught'red**
N. 31 **naked** exposed, as to an enemy. 33 **mean** of low birth.
37 **God's substitute** i.e. Richard. 38 **anointed** with holy oil, in
the coronation ceremony. 40 **may** can, must. 42 **Where** to whom.
then, alas, may Q (Devonshire, Petworth); Q (Huth, Capell),
other Qq, F *then may* N. 43 **God** Qq; F *heauen* (see I.1.187 N).

12

Duchess. Why then, I will. Farewell, old Gaunt.
Thou goest to Coventry, there to behold   45
Our cousin Herford and fell Mowbray fight.
O, sit my husband's wrongs on Herford's spear,
That it may enter butcher Mowbray's breast!
Or if misfortune miss the first career,
Be Mowbray's sins so heavy in his bosom   50
That they may break his foaming courser's back
And throw the rider headlong in the lists,
A caitiff recreant to my cousin Herford!
Farewell, old Gaunt. Thy sometimes brother's wife
With her companion, Grief, must end her life.   55
     Gaunt. Sister, farewell; I must to Coventry.
As much good stay with thee, as go with me.
     Duchess. Yet one word more. Grief boundeth where
          it falls,
Not with the empty hollowness, but weight.
I take my leave before I have begun,   60
For sorrow ends not when it seemeth done.
Commend me to thy brother, Edmund York.
Lo, this is all. Nay, yet depart not so.
Though this be all, do not so quickly go.
I shall remember more. Bid him—ah, what?—   65
With all good speed at Plashie visit me.

44 Why then . . . Gaunt N. 46 cousin Hereford was her nephew
and brother-in-law N. 49 misfortune i.e. to Mowbray. career
charge (a technical term in jousting). 53 caitiff recreant to a
false and wretched coward vanquished by. 54 sometimes sometime, former. 55 end live out. 58–9 Grief . . . weight N. 58 it
Q2; Q *is.* 59 empty Q (Devonshire, Petworth), other Qq; Q
(Huth, Capell), F *emptines.* 60 begun i.e. begun my lamenting.
62 thy other Qq, F *my.* 66 Plashie Qq, F; Pleshy, Gloucester's
country residence in Essex.

Alack, and what shall good old York there see
But empty lodgings and unfurnish'd walls,
Unpeopled offices, untrodden stones?   69
And what hear there for welcome but my groans?
Therefore commend me. Let him not come there
To seek out sorrow that dwells everywhere.
Desolate, desolate, will I hence and die.
The last leave of thee takes my weeping eye. *Exeunt*.

SCENE 3

*Enter the Lord Marshal and the Duke of
Aumerle.*

Marshal. My lord Aumerle, is Harry Herford
    arm'd?
Aumerle. Yea, at all points, and longs to enter in.
Marshal. The Duke of Norfolk, sprightfully and
    bold,
Stays but the summons of the appellant's trumpet.
Aumerle. Why, then, the champions are prepar'd,
    and stay   5
For nothing but his majesty's approach.

*The trumpets sound and the King enters with his
nobles [Gaunt, Bushy, Bagot, Green, and others].
When they are set, enter [Mowbray,] the Duke*

68 **unfurnish'd** not hung with tapestries (or possibly without
furniture). 70 **hear** Q (Devonshire, Petworth), other Qq, F;
Q (Huth, Capell) *cheere*. 73 **Desolate** disyllabic. **will I hence** I
will hence. SD **Marshal** on this occasion, the Duke of Surrey.
Aumerle on this occasion, High Constable of England. 3 **sprightfully and bold** with spirit and courage. 4 **the appellant's** read 'th'
appellant's' (also in l. 52). SD **enter Mowbray**, N.

14

of Norfolk in arms, defendant [, and herald].

King Richard. Marshal, demand of yonder
    champion
The cause of his arrival here in arms.
Ask him his name, and orderly proceed
To swear him in the justice of his cause.   10
    Marshal. In God's name and the king's, say who
        thou art,
And why thou com'st thus knightly clad in arms,
Against what man thou com'st, and what thy
        quarrel.
Speak truly on thy knighthood and thy oath,
As so defend thee heaven and thy valor!   15
    Mowbray. My name is Thomas Mowbray, Duke of
        Norfolk,
Who hither come engaged by my oath—
Which God defend a knight should violate!—
Both to defend my loyalty and truth
To God, my king, and my succeeding issue   20
Against the Duke of Herford that appeals me;
And, by the grace of God and this mine arm,
To prove him, in defending of myself,
A traitor to my God, my king, and me.
And as I truly fight, defend me heaven!   25

*The trumpets sound. Enter [Bullingbrooke,] the
    Duke of Herford, appellant, in armor [, and
        herald].*

King Richard. Marshal, ask yonder knight in arms

---

7 champion trisyllabic. **9 orderly** according to rule. **10 swear him
in** have him take an oath as to. **11 say who thou art** N. **13 quarrel**
complaint (a legal term). **15 As so defend** N. **18 defend** forbid
(compare French *défendre*). **20 my succeeding** N.

Both who he is and why he cometh hither
Thus plated in habiliments of war;
And formally according to our law,
Depose him in the justice of his cause.   30
 Marshal. What is thy name? And wherefore com'st
  thou hither
Before King Richard in his royal lists?
Against whom comest thou? And what's thy quarrel?
Speak like a true knight, so defend thee heaven!
 Bullingbrooke. Harry of Herford, Lancaster, and
  Darby   35
Am I, who ready here do stand in arms
To prove, by God's grace and my body's valor,
In lists, on Thomas Mowbray, Duke of Norfolk,
That he is a traitor, foul and dangerous,
To God of heaven, King Richard, and to me.   40
And as I truly fight, defend me heaven.
 Marshal. On pain of death, no person be so bold
Or daring-hardy as to touch the lists,
Except the Marshal and such officers
Appointed to direct these fair designs.   45
 Bullingbrooke. Lord Marshal, let me kiss my sover-
  eign's hand
And bow my knee before his majesty;
For Mowbray and myself are like two men
That vow a long and weary pilgrimage.
Then let us take a ceremonious leave   50

---

28 **plated** clad in plate armor; F *placed.* 30 **Depose** take his sworn
statement (deposition). 33 **comest** Q5; other Qq *comes;* F *com'st.*
35 **Darby** Derby (pronounced 'Darby'). 39 **he is** read 'he's' as F.
43 **daring-hardy** one of Shakespeare's compounded adjectives;
Qq *daring, hardy;* F *daring hardie.* 49 **vow . . . pilgrimage** ironic
prophecy of the double exile.

And loving farewell of our several friends.

Marshal. The appellant in all duty greets your
    highness
And craves to kiss your hand and take his leave.

King Richard. We will descend and fold him in our
    arms.
Cousin of Herford, as thy cause is right,   55
So be thy fortune in this royal fight!
Farewell, my blood; which if today thou shed,
Lament we may, but not revenge thee dead.

Bullingbrooke. O, let no noble eye profane a tear
For me if I be gor'd with Mowbray's spear.   60
As confident as is the falcon's flight
Against a bird, do I with Mowbray fight.
My loving lord, I take my leave of you,
Of you, my noble cousin, Lord Aumerle;
Not sick, although I have to do with death,   65
But lusty, young, and cheerly drawing breath.
Lo, as at English feasts, so I regreet
The daintiest last, to make the end most sweet.
O thou, the earthly author of my blood,
Whose youthful spirit, in me regenerate,   70
Doth with a twofold vigor lift me up
To reach at victory above my head,
Add proof unto mine armor with thy prayers,
And with thy blessings steel my lance's point,
That it may enter Mowbray's waxen coat   75
And furbish new the name of John a Gaunt

---

51 **several friends** friends one by one, or respective friends. 57
blood kinsman. 66 **cheerly** cheerily. 67 **regreet** greet. 70 **spirit**
monosyllabic. **regenerate** regenerated. 73 **proof** capacity to resist
weapons. 75 **waxen** i.e. easy to penetrate. 76 **furbish new** add new
glory or luster to; F *furnish new.* **a Gaunt** o' (of) Gaunt.

Even in the lusty havior of his son.

  Gaunt. God in thy good cause make thee pros-
     perous!
Be swift like lightning in the execution,
And let thy blows, doubly redoubled,   80
Fall like amazing thunder on the casque
Of thy adverse pernicious enemy.
Rouse up thy youthful blood; be valiant and live.

  Bullingbrooke. Mine innocence and Saint George
     to thrive!   84

  Mowbray. However God or fortune cast my lot,
There lives or dies, true to King Richard's throne,
A loyal, just, and upright gentleman.
Never did captive with a freer heart
Cast off his chains of bondage and embrace
His golden uncontroll'd enfranchisement,   90
More than my dancing soul doth celebrate
This feast of battle with mine adversary.
Most mighty liege, and my companion peers,
Take from my mouth the wish of happy years.
As gentle and as jocund as to jest   95
Go I to fight. Truth hath a quiet breast.

  King Richard. Farewell, my lord. Securely I espy
Virtue with valor couched in thine eye.
Order the trial, Marshal, and begin.

  Marshal. Harry of Herford, Lancaster, and
     Darby,   100
Receive thy lance, and God defend the right!

---

80 **redoubled** four syllables. 82 **adverse** stressed — $\underline{\prime}$; F *amaz'd*
(probably a printer's error). 83 **Rouse . . . live** an alexandrine.
84 **Mine . . . George** N. **thrive** i.e. make me victorious. 90
enfranchisement release. 95 **gentle** calm. **jest** play, sport. 97
Securely confidently (or possibly modifying *couched*).
  18

Bullingbrooke. Strong as a tower in hope, I cry amen.

Marshal. Go bear this lance to Thomas, Duke of Norfolk.

1. Herald. Harry of Herford, Lancaster, and Darby

Stands here for God, his sovereign, and himself,   105

On pain to be found false and recreant,

To prove the Duke of Norfolk, Thomas Mowbray,

A traitor to his God, his king, and him,

And dares him to set forward to the fight.

2. Herald. Here standeth Thomas Mowbray, Duke of Norfolk,   110

On pain to be found false and recreant,

Both to defend himself and to approve

Henry of Herford, Lancaster, and Darby

To God, his sovereign, and to him disloyal,

Courageously and with a free desire   115

Attending but the signal to begin.

Marshal. Sound trumpets and set forward combatants.   [*A charge sounded.*]

Stay! The king hath thrown his warder down.

King Richard. Let them lay by their helmets and their spears

And both return back to their chairs again.   120

Withdraw with us, and let the trumpets sound

While we return these dukes what we decree.

[*A long flourish.*]

---

108 **his God** Q (Devonshire, Petworth), other Qq, F; Q (Capell, Huth) *God.* 112 **approve** prove. 118 **warder** staff. **down** i.e. to stop the contest. 122 **While . . . decree** until I announce to these dukes my decision.

Draw near,
And list what with our council we have done.
For that our kingdom's earth should not be soil'd
With that dear blood which it hath fostered;   126
And for our eyes do hate the dire aspect
Of civil wounds plough'd up with neighbors' sword;
And for we think the eagle-winged pride
Of sky-aspiring and ambitious thoughts   130
With rival-hating envy set on you
To wake our peace, which in our country's cradle
Draws the sweet infant breath of gentle sleep;
Which so rous'd up with boist'rous untun'd drums,
With harsh-resounding trumpets' dreadful bray
And grating shock of wrathful iron arms,   136
Might from our quiet confines fright fair peace
And make us wade even in our kinred's blood;
Therefore we banish you our territories.
You, cousin Herford, upon pain of life,   140
Till twice five summers have enrich'd our fields,
Shall not regreet our fair dominions
But tread the stranger paths of banishment.
  Bullingbrooke. Your will be done. This must my
        comfort be—   144
That sun that warms you here shall shine on me,

123–4 **Draw . . . list** one line in Q, F. 123 **Draw near** the short
line gives the dukes time to approach. 125 **For that** in order that.
127 **for** because. **aspect** stressed — $\stackrel{\prime}{\smile}$. 128 **civil** Q (Devonshire,
Petworth), other Qq, F; Q (Huth, Capell) *cruell*. 129–33 **And for**
. . . **sleep** not in F. 131 **envy** enmity. **set on you** set you on.
132 **wake** disturb. 133 **infant** . . . **sleep** i.e. peace of short dura-
tion. 134 **Which** antecedent: *sleep.* **untun'd** discordant. 137 **confines** territories. 142 **regreet** salute again (unlike I.3.67). **dominions** four syllables. 143 **stranger** foreign.

And those his golden beams to you here lent
Shall point on me and gild my banishment.
   King Richard. Norfolk, for thee remains a heavier
     doom,
Which I with some unwillingness pronounce:
The sly slow hours shall not determinate   150
The dateless limit of thy dear exile.
The hopeless word of 'never to return'
Breathe I against thee, upon pain of life.
   Mowbray. A heavy sentence, my most sovereign
     liege,   154
And all unlook'd for from your highness' mouth.
A dearer merit, not so deep a maim
As to be cast forth in the common air,
Have I deserved at your highness' hands.
The language I have learnt these forty years,
My native English, now I must forgo;   160
And now my tongue's use is to me no more
Than an unstringed viol or a harp,
Or like a cunning instrument cas'd up
Or, being open, put into his hands
That knows no touch to tune the harmony.   165
Within my mouth you have enjail'd my tongue,
Doubly portcullis'd with my teeth and lips;
And dull, unfeeling, barren ignorance
Is made my jailer to attend on me.
I am too old to fawn upon a nurse,   170
Too far in years to be a pupil now.
What is thy sentence then but speechless death,

148 **doom** sentence. 150 **determinate** set a limit to (a legal term).
151 **dear** grievous. **exile** stressed — ⏝ (also in l. 217). 159 **forty**
a round figure (Mowbray is nearer thirty now). 163 **cunning** i.e.
made and played with skill. 165 **That** who. 172 **then** F; not in Qq.

Which robs my tongue from breathing native
    breath?
  King Richard. It boots thee not to be compassion-
    ate.
After our sentence plaining comes too late.   175
  Mowbray. Then thus I turn me from my country's
    light
To dwell in solemn shades of endless night.
  King Richard. Return again, and take an oath
    with thee.
Lay on our royal sword your banish'd hands,
Swear by the duty that you owe to God—   180
Our part therein we banish with yourselves—
To keep the oath that we administer:
You never shall, so help you truth and God,
Embrace each other's love in banishment;
Nor never look upon each other's face;   185
Nor never write, regreet, nor reconcile
This low'ring tempest of your home-bred hate;
Nor never by advised purpose meet
To plot, contrive, or complot any ill   189
'Gainst us, our state, our subjects, or our land.
  Bullingbrooke. I swear.
  Mowbray. And I, to keep all this.
  Bullingbrooke. Norfolk, so far as to mine enemy:
By this time, had the king permitted us,
One of our souls had wand'red in the air,   195
Banish'd this frail sepulcher of our flesh
As now our flesh is banish'd from this land.

---

173 Which antecedent: *thy sentence.* 174 compassionate appealing
for pity. 179 on . . . sword i.e. on the cross hilt (also forms a
Christian cross). 180 you owe F; Qq *y'owe.* 181 Our part therein
my share in your duty. 193 so far . . . enemy N. 196 sepulcher
stressed — ´ —.

ember me what a deal of world	
n the jewels that I love.	270
erve a long apprenticehood	
assages, and in the end,	
reedom, boast of nothing else	
as a journeyman to grief?	
laces that the eye of heaven visits	275
e man ports and happy havens.	
cessity to reason thus:	
irtue like necessity.	
e king did banish thee,	
king. Woe doth the heavier sit	280
ceives it is but faintly borne.	
t thee forth to purchase honor,	
king exil'd thee. Or suppose	
stilence hangs in our air	
flying to a fresher clime.	285
y soul holds dear, imagine it	
ay thou goest, not whence thou com'st.	
inging birds musicians,	
hereon thou tread'st the presence	
ir ladies, and thy steps no more	290
tful measure or a dance;	
sorrow hath less power to bite	
mocks at it and sets it light.	
e. O, who can hold a fire in his hand	

. . world remind me how far. 272 passages
ourneyman artisan (also a quibble for 'traveler'
275–6 heaven . . . havens a pun (the words
alike). 283 exil'd stressed — ⌣. 288 musicians
strow'd strewed N. 291 measure stately dance,
292 gnarling snarling, growling. 294 fire di-

Confess thy treasons ere thou fly the realm.
Since thou hast far to go, bear not along
The clogging burthen of a guilty soul.   200
   Mowbray. No, Bullingbrooke. If ever I were traitor,
My name be blotted from the book of life
And I from heaven banish'd as from hence!
But what thou art, God, thou, and I do know,
And all too soon, I fear, the king shall rue.   205
Farewell, my liege. Now no way can I stray.
Save back to England, all the world's my way. *Exit.*
   King Richard. Uncle, even in the glasses of thine eyes
I see thy grieved heart. Thy sad aspect
Hath from the number of his banish'd years   210
Pluck'd four away. [*To Bullingbrooke.*] Six frozen winters spent,
Return with welcome home from banishment.
   Bullingbrooke. How long a time lies in one little word!
Four lagging winters and four wanton springs
End in a word. Such is the breath of kings.   215
   Gaunt. I thank my liege that in regard of me
He shortens four years of my son's exile.
But little vantage shall I reap thereby,
For eare the six years that he hath to spend   219
Can change their moons and bring their times about,
My oil-dried lamp and time-bewasted light
Shall be extinct with age and endless night,
My inch of taper will be burnt and done,

200 burthen burden. 202 blotted . . . life compare Revelation
3:5. 208 glasses mirrors. 209 aspect stressed — ⌣. 211 Pluck'd
four away N. 214 wanton luxuriant (sportive, possibly). 219 eare
e'er (ever). 220 bring their times about cause their seasons to come
around. 222 night Q4, F; Q *nightes.*

And blindfold Death not let me see my son.
King Richard. Why, uncle, thou hast many years
    to live.   225
Gaunt. But not a minute, king, that thou canst
    give.
Shorten my days thou canst with sullen sorrow
And pluck nights from me, but not lend a morrow.
Thou canst help time to furrow me with age,
But stop no wrinkle in his pilgrimage.   230
Thy word is current with him for my death,
But dead, thy kingdom cannot buy my breath.
King Richard. Thy son is banish'd upon good
    advice,
Whereto thy tongue a party-verdict gave.
Why at our justice seem'st thou then to lower? 235
Gaunt. Things sweet to taste prove in digestion
    sour.
You urg'd me as a judge, but I had rather
You would have bid me argue like a father.
O, had it been a stranger, not my child,   239
To smooth his fault I should have been more mild.
A partial slander sought I to avoid,
And in the sentence my own life destroy'd.
Alas, I look'd when some of you should say
I was too strict to make mine own away,
But you gave leave to my unwilling tongue   245
Against my will to do myself this wrong.
King Richard. Cousin, farewell; and, uncle, bid
    him so.

231 is current passes current, is valid. him i.e. time. 233 good
advice full consideration. 234 party-verdict assent. 239–42 O . . .
destroy'd not in F. 240 To smooth in palliating. 241 partial
slander charge of bias. sought Q (Devonshire, Huth), Q3–5;
Q (Capell, Petworth), Q2 *ought.*

Six years we banish[
[*Flourish.*]
Aumerle. Cousin,
    not know,
From where you d
Marshal. My lord
As far as land wil
Gaunt. O, to wh
    words
That thou return'
Bullingbrooke. I
    you,
When the tongue'
To breathe the al
Gaunt. Thy grie
Bullingbrooke. J
    time.
Gaunt. What is
Bullingbrooke. T
    hour ten.
Gaunt. Call it a
Bullingbrooke.
    it so,
Which finds it an
Gaunt. The sull
Esteem as foil w
The precious je
Bullingbrooke.
    make

SD Flourish . . . t
abundant read 'th' a
Elizabethan spelling
finds. 265 sullen slo
confusion of *f* and

Will but re
I wander fro
Must I not
To foreign
Having my
But that I
Gaunt. All
And to a wis
Teach thy
There is no
Think not t
But thou the
Where it pe
Go, say I se
And not the
Devouring p
And thou ar
Look what t
To lie that
Suppose the
The grass
    strow'd,
The flowers
Than a delig
For gnarling
The man tha
Bullingbroo

269 remember
wanderings. 274
as 'journeyer').
were pronounced
four syllables. 28
or dancing figur
syllabic.

By thinking on the frosty Caucasus?   295
Or cloy the hungry edge of appetite
By bare imagination of a feast?
Or wallow naked in December snow
By thinking on fantastic summer's heat?
O, no! The apprehension of the good   300
Gives but the greater feeling to the worse.
Fell Sorrow's tooth doth never rankle more
Than when he bites, but lanceth not the sore.
   Gaunt. Come, come, my son, I'll bring thee on thy
    way.
Had I thy youth and cause, I would not stay.   305
   Bullingbrooke. Then, England's ground, farewell;
    sweet soil, adieu,
My mother, and my nurse, that bears me yet.
Where eare I wander, boast of this I can,
Though banish'd, yet a trueborn Englishman.
Exeunt.

SCENE 4

*Enter the King with [Green and Bagot] at one
door, and the Lord Aumerle at another.*

   King Richard. We did observe. Cousin Aumerle,
How far brought you high Herford on his way?
   Aumerle. I brought high Herford, if you call him
    so,
But to the next highway, and there I left him.

299 fantastic imaginary. 301 greater . . . worse greater poig-
nancy to evil things. 302 rankle inflict a festering wound (OED).
303 he other Qq, F *it.* SD Green and Bagot N. 4 highway a pun
on *high* (l. 3) as 'proud' or 'main.'

King Richard. And say, what store of parting tears
    were shed?   5
  Aumerle. Faith, none for me, except the northeast
    wind
Which then blew bitterly against our faces,
Awak'd the sleeping rheum, and so by chance
Did grace our hollow parting with a tear.
  King Richard. What said our cousin when you
    parted with him?   10
  Aumerle. 'Farewell.'
And for my heart disdained that my tongue
Should so profane the word, that taught me craft
To counterfeit oppression of such grief
That words seem'd buried in my sorrow's grave. 15
Marry, would the word 'farewell' have length'ned
    hours
And added years to his short banishment,
He should have had a volume of farewells;
But since it would not, he had none of me.
  King Richard. He is our cousin, cousin; but 'tis
    doubt,   20
When time shall call him home from banishment,
Whether our kinsman come to see his friends.
Ourself and Bushy here, Bagot and Green,
Observ'd his courtship to the common people—
How he did seem to dive into their hearts 25
With humble and familiar courtesy;

5 store abundance. 6 **Faith** in faith. **for me** for my part. 7 **blew**
F *grew.* 8 **sleeping** F *sleepie.* **rheum** tears. 11–12 **Farewell . . .
tongue** one line in Q, F. 12 **for** because. 13 **that** i.e. my heart's
disdain. 16 **Marry** indeed, to be sure (originally an oath in the
name of the Virgin Mary). 19 **of** from. 20 **cousin, cousin** Q *Coosens
Coosin;* F *Cosin (Cosin).* 20–2 **doubt . . . friends** N. 23 **Ourself
. . . Green** N.

28

What reverence he did throw away on slaves,
Wooing poor craftsmen with the craft of smiles
And patient underbearing of his fortune,
As 'twere to banish their affects with him.   30
Off goes his bonnet to an oyster-wench;
A brace of draymen bid God speed him well
And had the tribute of his supple knee,
With 'Thanks, my countrymen, my loving friends,'
As were our England in reversion his,   35
And he our subjects' next degree in hope.
    Green. Well, he is gone, and with him go these
        thoughts.
Now for the rebels which stand out in Ireland
Expedient manage must be made, my liege,
Ere further leisure yield them further means   40
For their advantage and your highness' loss.
    King Richard. We will ourself in person to this
        war;
And, for our coffers, with too great a court
And liberal largess, are grown somewhat light,
We are enforc'd to farm our royal realm,   45
The revenue whereof shall furnish us
For our affairs in hand. If that come short,
Our substitutes at home shall have blank charters,
Whereto, when they shall know what men are rich,
They shall subscribe them for large sums of gold   50

27 **What** Q (Devonshire, Huth), F; Q (Capell, Petworth), other
Qq *With.* 28 **smiles** F *soules.* 29 **underbearing** endurance. 30
their affects i.e. the affection of the common people. 35 **reversion**
right of future possession. 36 **next degree in hope** choice for heir
presumptive. 39 **Expedient manage** expeditious arrangements.
43 **great** large and costly. 43–4 **court . . . largess** N. 45 **farm
. . . realm** N. 48 **substitutes** deputies. 50 **subscribe them** fill in
the amount to be paid (see l. 45 N).

And send them after to supply our wants,
For we will make for Ireland presently.

Enter Bushy.

Bushy, what news?
  Bushy. Old John of Gaunt is grievous sick, my
    lord,
Suddenly taken, and hath sent posthaste   55
To entreat your majesty to visit him.
  King Richard. Where lies he?
  Bushy. At Ely House.
  King Richard. Now put it, God, in the physician's
    mind
To help him to his grave immediately!   60
The lining of his coffers shall make coats
To deck our soldiers for these Irish wars.
Come, gentlemen, let's all go visit him.
Pray God we may make haste, and come too late!
  All. Amen.   *Exeunt* 65

51 them i.e. large sums. 52 **presently** immediately. SD **Enter
Bushy** Qq *Enter Bushie with newes.* 53 **Bushy, what news** N.
54 **grievous** F *verie.* 58 **Ely House** Bishop of Ely's palace in
London. 61 **coats** i.e. of mail. 65 **All** not in Qq, F.

Act II

SCENE 1

Enter John of Gaunt, sick, with the Duke of York, etc.

Gaunt. Will the king come, that I may breathe
my last
In wholesome counsel to his unstaid youth?

York. Vex not yourself, nor strive nor with your
breath,
For all in vain comes counsel to his ear.   4

Gaunt. O, but they say the tongues of dying men
Enforce attention like deep harmony.
Where words are scarce they are seldom spent in
vain,
For they breathe truth that breathe their words in
pain.
He that no more must say is listen'd more
  Than they whom youth and ease have taught to
  glose.   10
More are men's ends mark'd than their lives before.
  The setting sun, and music at the close,
As the last taste of sweets, is sweetest last,
Writ in remembrance more than things long past.
Though Richard my live's counsel would not hear,

2 **unstaid** stressed — ⌣ ´. 9–12 **He that . . . close** a quatrain.
10 **glose** speak flatteringly. 12 **close** final cadences. 13 **As** like.
15 **live's** old genitive form.

31

My death's sad tale may yet undeaf his ear. 16
  York. No, it is stopp'd with other flattering sounds,
As praises, of whose taste the wise are fond,
Lascivious meters, to whose venom sound
The open ear of youth doth always listen— 20
Report of fashions in proud Italy,
Whose manners still our tardy apish nation
Limps after in base imitation.
Where doth the world thrust forth a vanity—
So it be new, there's no respect how vile— 25
That is not quickly buzz'd into his ears?
Then all too late comes counsel to be heard
Where will doth mutiny with wit's regard.
Direct not him whose way himself will choose.
'Tis breath thou lack'st, and that breath wilt thou
    lose. 30
  Gaunt. Methinks I am a prophet new inspir'd
And thus expiring do foretell of him.
His rash fierce blaze of riot cannot last,
For violent fires soon burn out themselves;
Small showers last long, but sudden storms are
    short. 35
He tires betimes that spurs too fast betimes,
With eager feeding food doth choke the feeder.

16 My . . . tale i.e. of Gaunt dying. 17 flattering disyllabic;
hence F *flatt'ring*. 18 of whose . . . fond N. 19 meters songs.
venom venomous. 21 proud gorgeous, and corrupting. 22 still
ever. tardy apish unenterprising and imitative. 23 imitation five
syllables. 25 So if, provided that. there's no respect it matters
not. 26 buzz'd whispered (a contemptuous word). 28 with wit's
regard against good judgment. 31–2 inspir'd . . . expiring a
quibble. 33 rash fast kindled and fast burning. riot riotous living.
34 violent fires both disyllabic. 35 showers monosyllabic. 36
betimes soon, early.

Light vanity, insatiate cormorant,
Consuming means, soon preys upon itself.
This royal throne of kings, this scept'red isle,   40
This earth of majesty, this seat of Mars,
This other Eden, demiparadise,
This fortress built by Nature for herself
Against infection and the hand of war,
This happy breed of men, this little world,   45
This precious stone set in the silver sea,
Which serves it in the office of a wall
Or as a moat defensive to a house
Against the envy of less happier lands;
This blessed plot, this earth, this realm, this Eng-
     land,   50
This nurse, this teeming womb of royal kings,
Fear'd by their breed and famous by their birth,
Renowned for their deeds as far from home,
For Christian service and true chivalry,
As is the sepulcher in stubborn Jewry   55
Of the world's ransom, blessed Mary's son;
This land of such dear souls, this dear dear land,
Dear for her reputation through the world,
Is now leas'd out—I die pronouncing it—
Like to a tenement or pelting farm.   60

38 insatiate insatiable. 39 means i.e. money. 40–55 This royal
. . . Jewry N. 41 earth England as an earth or world (l. 45) in
itself. 44 infection pestilence (or possibly a moral word). 45 breed
race, or brood. little world Elizabethan microcosm. 47 office
function. 48 as a Q4, Q5, F; other Qq as. 49 envy enmity. 52.
Fear'd inspiring fear. 54 For . . . chivalry almost parenthetical.
55 stubborn ruthless, or stubborn about accepting Christianity.
Jewry Judea. 56 Of the world's ransom of the Savior who re-
deemed the world. 60 tenement real estate held by a tenant.
pelting paltry.

England, bound in with the triumphant sea,
Whose rocky shore beats back the envious siege
Of wat'ry Neptune, is now bound in with shame,
With inky blots and rotten parchment bonds.
That England that was wont to conquer others   65
Hath made a shameful conquest of itself.
Ah, would the scandal vanish with my life,
How happy then were my ensuing death!

Enter King, Queen [, *Aumerle, Bushy, Green,
Bagot, Ross, and Willoughby*].

York. The king is come. Deal mildly with his youth,
For young hot colts being rag'd do rage the more.
   Queen. How fares our noble uncle Lancaster?   71
   King Richard. What comfort, man? How is't with
     aged Gaunt?
   Gaunt. O, how that name befits my composition!
Old Gaunt indeed, and gaunt in being old.
Within me Grief hath kept a tedious fast,   75
And who abstains from meat that is not gaunt?
For sleeping England long time have I watch'd;
Watching breeds leanness, leanness is all gaunt.
The pleasure that some fathers feed upon   79
Is my strict fast—I mean my children's looks—
And therein fasting hast thou made me gaunt.
Gaunt am I for the grave, gaunt as a grave,
Whose hollow womb inherits naught but bones.

---

64 inky . . . bonds contemptuous expression for written deeds.
SD Enter . . . Willoughby N. 69 youth Richard was thirty-two.
70 rag'd enraged N. 71 Queen Richard's child-wife Isabelle.
72 What comfort i.e. 'do you feel better?' 73–83 O, how . . .
bones a series of puns on *gaunt* N. 73 composition bodily condition. 77 watch'd kept awake. 81 therein fasting modifies *me*.

King Richard. Can sick men play so nicely with
　　their names?

Gaunt. No, misery makes sport to mock itself.　　85
Since thou dost seek to kill my name in me,
I mock my name, great king, to flatter thee.

King Richard. Should dying men flatter with those
　　that live?

Gaunt. No, no, men living flatter those that die.

King Richard. Thou, now a-dying, say'st thou
　　flatter'st me.　　90

Gaunt. O, no! Thou diest, though I the sicker be.

King Richard. I am in health, I breathe, and see
　　thee ill.

Gaunt. Now He that made me knows I see thee ill—
Ill in myself to see, and in thee seeing ill.
Thy deathbed is no lesser than thy land,　　95
Wherein thou liest in reputation sick;
And thou, too careless patient as thou art,
Committ'st thy anointed body to the cure
Of those physicians that first wounded thee.
A thousand flatterers sit within thy crown,　　100
Whose compass is no bigger than thy head,
And yet, incaged in so small a verge,
The waste is no whit lesser than thy land.
O, had thy grandsire with a prophet's eye

---

84 **nicely** subtly, fancifully. 86 **to kill . . . me** i.e. by banishing
his son. 89 **those that die** i.e. Richard (see l. 95). 91 **diest** monosyllabic. 93 **ill** evil and dimly. 94 **Ill . . . ill** N. 95–6 **Thy . . .
sick** N. 96 **liest** monosyllabic. 98 **thy anointed** three syllables;
F *thy' anointed.* 99 **those physicians** i.e. Richard's corrupt favorites. 100–13 **A thousand . . . king** N. 100 **crown** both head and
diadem. 102 **incaged** F; Qq *inraged.* **verge** boundary (a legal
term). 103 **waste** destruction (here a legal term). 104 **grandsire**
Edward III.

Seen how his son's son should destroy his sons,   105
From forth thy reach he would have laid thy shame,
Deposing thee before thou wert possess'd,
Which art possess'd now to depose thyself.
Why, cousin, wert thou regent of the world,
It were a shame to let this land by lease;   110
But for thy world enjoying but this land,
Is it not more than shame to shame it so?
Landlord of England art thou now, not king.
Thy state of law is bondslave to the law,   114
And thou—

    King Richard.   A lunatic lean-witted fool,
Presuming on an ague's privilege,
Dar'st with thy frozen admonition
Make pale our cheek, chasing the royal blood
With fury from his native residence.
Now, by my seat's right royal majesty,   120
Wert thou not brother to great Edward's son,
This tongue that runs so roundly in thy head
Should run thy head from thy unreverent shoulders.

    Gaunt. O, spare me not, my brother Edward's son,
For that I was his father Edward's son!   125
That blood already, like the pelican,
Hast thou tapp'd out and drunkenly carous'd.
My brother Gloucester, plain well-meaning soul—

105 his son's the Black Prince's. his sons Gloucester and Gaunt
himself. 107 possess'd i.e. of the throne. 108 Which who. possess'd i.e. by a mad impulse (originally by a devil). depose
thyself i.e. be ruled by favorites. 111 But . . . land N. 113 now,
not other Qq *now not, not;* Q5 *now not, nor;* F *and not.* 114 state
of law legal status. 115 And thou . . . lunatic N. lean-witted
gaunt-witted? (see l. 78). 117 admonition five syllables. 119 his
its. 122 roundly glibly (also a pun). 124 brother other Qq; Q, F
brothers. 126 like the pelican N. 127 carous'd drunk down in
large drafts.

Whom fair befall in heaven 'mongst happy souls!—
May be a precedent and witness good   130
That thou respect'st not spilling Edward's blood.
Join with the present sickness that I have,
And thy unkindness be like crooked age,
To crop at once a too long wither'd flower.
Live in thy shame, but die not shame with thee!   135
These words hereafter thy tormentors be!
Convey me to my bed, then to my grave.
Love they to live that love and honor have.

              Exit [*borne off by his attendants*].
  King Richard. And let them die that age and sullens
    have,
For both hast thou, and both become the grave.   140
  York. I do beseech your majesty, impute his words
To wayward sickliness and age in him.
He loves you, on my life, and holds you dear
As Harry Duke of Herford, were he here.
  King Richard. Right, you say true. As Herford's
    love, so his;   145
As theirs, so mine; and all be as it is.

        [*Enter Northumberland.*]

  Northumberland. My liege, old Gaunt commends
    him to your majesty.
  King Richard. What says he?
  Northumberland.   Nay, nothing; all is
    said.

130 **precedent** proof or example. 131 **respect'st not** do not scruple
about. 133 **crooked** as with a sickle? (see l. 134). 139 **sullens**
melancholy. 140 **become** are fit for. 145–6 **As . . . mine** N.
147 **Northumberland** i.e. Hotspur's father, Henry Percy, Earl of
Northumberland. **him** himself. 148–214 **Nay, nothing . . . good**
for Holinshed's version see Appendix B.

His tongue is now a stringless instrument.
Words, life, and all, old Lancaster hath spent.　150

York. Be York the next that must be bankrout so!
Though death be poor, it ends a mortal woe.

King Richard. The ripest fruit first falls, and so
　　doth he.
His time is spent, our pilgrimage must be.
So much for that. Now for our Irish wars.　155
We must supplant those rough rug-headed kerns
Which live like venom where no venom else
But only they have privilege to live.
And for these great affairs do ask some charge,
Towards our assistance we do seize to us　160
The plate, coin, revenues, and moveables
Whereof our uncle Gaunt did stand possess'd.

York. How long shall I be patient? Ah, how long
Shall tender duty make me suffer wrong?　164
Not Gloucester's death, nor Herford's banishment,
Nor Gaunt's rebukes, nor England's private wrongs,
Nor the prevention of poor Bullingbrooke
About his marriage, nor my own disgrace,
Have ever made me sour my patient cheek
Or bend one wrinkle on my sovereign's face.　170

---

149 tongue . . . instrument compare I.3.161–2. 151 bankrout
bankrupt; F *bankrupt*. 154 our pilgrimage must be i.e. we must
live on. 156 supplant uproot, drive out. rug-headed kerns shaggy-
haired Irish foot soldiers. kerns Q (Huth), Q3–5, F; Q (Capell,
Petworth, Devonshire), Q2 *kerne* (which may be collective here).
157–8 Which . . . live refers to legend that St. Patrick rid Ireland of snakes. 159 for because. charge outlay. 164 tender scrupu-
lous, perhaps excessively so. 166 Gaunt's i.e. given to Gaunt
(objective genitive). private suffered by private persons. 168
marriage . . . disgrace N. 170 bend one wrinkle on show one
sign of criticism before.

38

I am the last of noble Edward's sons,
Of whom thy father, Prince of Wales, was first.
In war was never lion rag'd more fierce,
In peace was never gentle lamb more mild,
Than was that young and princely gentleman.   175
His face thou hast, for even so look'd he,
Accomplish'd with the number of thy hours.
But when he frown'd, it was against the French
And not against his friends. His noble hand
Did win what he did spend, and spent not that   180
Which his triumphant father's hand had won.
His hands were guilty of no kinred blood,
But bloody with the enemies of his kin.
O Richard! York is too far gone with grief,
Or else he never would compare between.   185
    King Richard. Why, uncle, what the matter?
    York.   O my
        liege,
Pardon me, if you please; if not, I, pleas'd
Not to be pardon'd, am content withal.
Seek you to seize and gripe into your hands
The royalties and rights of banish'd Herford?   190
Is not Gaunt dead, and doth not Herford live?
Was not Gaunt just, and is not Harry true?
Did not the one deserve to have an heir?
Is not his heir a well-deserving son?
Take Herford's rights away, and take from time   195
His charters and his customary rights,

---

172 **Prince of Wales** Edward the Black Prince. 173 **lion** rag'd
lion that raged. 177 **Accomplish'd . . . hours** when your age
(i.e. thirty-two). **the** F; Qq *a*. 185 **compare between** draw com-
parisons (or perhaps the sentence is cut off). 186–8 **Why . . .
withal** N. 189 **gripe** grip. 190 **royalties** privileges. 195 **rights** i.e. of
making the son heir to the father.

Let not tomorrow then ensue today.
Be not thyself; for how art thou a king
But by fair sequence and succession?
Now, afore God—God forbid I say true!—   200
If you do wrongfully seize Herford's rights,
Call in the letters-patents that he hath
By his attorneys general to sue
His livery, and deny his off'red homage,
You pluck a thousand dangers on your head,   205
You lose a thousand well-disposed hearts,
And prick my tender patience to those thoughts
Which honor and allegiance cannot think.
   King Richard. Think what you will, we seize into
     our hands
His plate, his goods, his money, and his lands.   210
   York. I'll not be by the while. My liege, farewell.
What will ensue hereof there's none can tell,
But by bad courses may be understood
That their events can never fall out good.   *Exit.*
   King Richard. Go Bushy, to the Earl of Wiltshire
     straight.   215
Bid him repair to us to Ely House
To see this business. Tomorrow next
We will for Ireland; and 'tis time, I trow.
And we create, in absence of ourself,
Our uncle York Lord Governor of England,   220
For he is just and always lov'd us well.
Come on, our queen. Tomorrow must we part.

197 **ensue** follow (here transitive). 199 **succession** four syllables.
202 **letters-patents** N. 203–4 **sue His livery** bring suit for delivery
(of his property). 207 **patience** self-control. 213 **by** concerning.
may it may. 215 **Earl of Wiltshire** Lord Treasurer of England.
217 **see** see to. **business** trisyllabic.

Be merry, for our time of stay is short.
        [*Flourish.*] *Exeunt. Manent Northumberland*
                [*,Willoughby, and Ross*].
Northumberland. Well, lords, the Duke of Lan-
    caster is dead.
Ross. And living too, for now his son is duke.   225
Willoughby. Barely in title, not in revenues.
Northumberland. Richly in both, if justice had her
    right.
Ross. My heart is great, but it must break with
    silence
Ear't be disburden'd with a liberal tongue.
Northumberland. Nay, speak thy mind, and let him
    nere speak more   230
That speaks thy words again to do thee harm!
Willoughby. Tends that thou wouldst speak to the
    Duke of Herford?
If it be so, out with it boldly, man.
Quick is mine ear to hear of good towards him.
Ross. No good at all that I can do for him,   235
Unless you call it good to pity him,
Bereft and gelded of his patrimony.
Northumberland. Now, afore God, 'tis shame such
    wrongs are borne
In him a royal prince and many mo
Of noble blood in this declining land.   240
The king is not himself, but basely led
By flatterers. And what they will inform,
Merely in hate, 'gainst any of us all,
That will the king severely prosecute
'Gainst us, our lives, our children, and our heirs.   245

229 **Ear't** before it. **liberal** disyllabic. 230 **nere** read 'ne'er'
(never). 232 **Tends . . . speak** does what you say refer? 239 **In
him** in his case (referring to *wrongs*). **mo** more.

41

Ross. The commons hath he pill'd with grievous
    taxes
And quite lost their hearts. The nobles hath he fin'd
For ancient quarrels and quite lost their hearts.

Willoughby. And daily new exactions are devis'd,
As blanks, benevolences, and I wot not what.   250
But what, a God's name, doth become of this?

Northumberland. Wars hath not wasted it, for
    warr'd he hath not,
But basely yielded upon compromise
That which his noble ancestors achiev'd with blows.
More hath he spent in peace than they in wars.   255

Ross. The Earl of Wiltshire hath the realm in farm.

Willoughby. The king's grown bankrout like a
    broken man.

Northumberland. Reproach and dissolution hangeth
    over him.

Ross. He hath not money for these Irish wars,
His burthenous taxations notwithstanding,   260
But by the robbing of the banish'd duke.

Northumberland. His noble kinsman. Most degen-
    erate king!
But, lords, we hear this fearful tempest sing,
Yet seek no shelter to avoid the storm.
We see the wind sit sore upon our sails,   265
And yet we strike not, but securely perish.

246 **pill'd** pillaged, plundered; F2; Qq *pild;* F *pil'd.* 250 **blanks**
blank charters (see I.4.48). **benevolences** forced loans or gifts;
read 'benev'lence.' 251 **a** in. **this** i.e. all this money. 252–4 **Wars**
. . . **blows** N. 252 **hath** a southern plural. 254 **That** . . . **blows**
an alexandrine. **noble** not in F. 256 **in farm** compare I.4.45.
257 **king's** Q3; Q *King;* F *Kings.* 258 **dissolution** destruction.
hangeth over read 'hang'th o'er.' 265 **sit sore** weigh heavily.
266 **strike not** lower not our sails (also a pun). **securely** heedlessly.

Ross. We see the very wrack that we must suffer,
And unavoided is the danger now
For suffering so the causes of our wrack.
   Northumberland. Not so. Even through the hollow
     eyes of death   270
I spy life peering, but I dare not say
How near the tidings of our comfort is.
   Willoughby. Nay, let us share thy thoughts as thou
     dost ours.
   Ross. Be confident to speak, Northumberland.
We three are but thyself, and, speaking so,   275
Thy words are but as thoughts. Therefore be bold.
   Northumberland. Then thus: I have from Le Port
     Blan, a bay
In Brittaine, receiv'd intelligence
That Harry Duke of Herford, Rainold Lord Cob-
     ham

.   280

That late broke from the Duke of Exeter,
His brother, Archbishop late of Canterbury,
Sir Thomas Erpingham, Sir John Ramston,
Sir John Norbery, Sir Robert Waterton, and Fran-
     cis Quoint;
All these well furnish'd by the Duke of Brittaine   285
With eight tall ships, three thousand men of war,
Are making hither with all due expedience

269 **suffering** disyllabic. 272 **tidings** a singular. 275 **are but thy-**
self are of the same mind. 277 **Le Port Blan** N. 277–8 **a bay** . . .
intelligence one line in Q, F. 278 **Brittaine** Q5, F *Britaine;* other
Qq *Brittanie.* 279 **Rainold** Reginald. 279–81 **Cobham** . . . **Exeter**
N. 283 **Sir John Ramston** more accurately, Sir Thomas Ramston.
284 **Quoint** N. 286 **men of war** soldiers.

And shortly mean to touch our northern shore.
Perhaps they had ere this, but that they stay
The first departing of the king for Ireland.   290
If then we shall shake off our slavish yoke,
Imp out our drooping country's broken wing,
Redeem from broking pawn the blemish'd crown,
Wipe off the dust that hides our scepter's gilt,
And make high majesty look like itself,   295
Away with me in post to Ravenspurgh.
But if you faint, as fearing to do so,
Stay and be secret, and myself will go.
   Ross. To horse, to horse! Urge doubts to them that
      fear.
   Willoughby. Hold out my horse, and I will first be
      there.   *Exeunt.*

SCENE 2

Enter the Queen, Bushy, Bagot.

   Bushy. Madam, your majesty is too much sad.
You promis'd, when you parted with the king,
To lay aside life-harming heaviness
And entertain a cheerful disposition.   4
   Queen. To please the king, I did; to please myself,
I cannot do it. Yet I know no cause
Why I should welcome such a guest as Grief,
Save bidding farewell to so sweet a guest

291 **shall** mean to. 292 **Imp out** repair (a term in falconry).
293 **broking pawn** pawn in the hands of brokers. 296 **in post** at
full speed. **Ravenspurgh** once the main port on the Humber.
297 **faint** are fainthearted. **as** though. 299 **Urge** mention. 300
Hold out my horse let my horse hold out. 3 **life-harming** Q3–5
halfe-harming; F *selfe-harming.* 4 **entertain** maintain.

As my sweet Richard. Yet again, methinks
Some unborn sorrow, ripe in Fortune's womb,   10
Is coming towards me, and my inward soul
With nothing trembles. At something it grieves
More than with parting from my lord the king.
  Bushy. Each substance of a grief hath twenty
    shadows,
Which shows like grief itself but is not so;   15
For Sorrow's eye, glazed with blinding tears,
Divides one thing entire to many objects—
Like perspectives which, rightly gaz'd upon,
Show nothing but confusion, ey'd awry,
Distinguish form. So your sweet majesty,   20
Looking awry upon your lord's departure,
Find shapes of grief more than himself to wail,
Which, look'd on as it is, is naught but shadows
Of what it is not. Then, thrice-gracious queen,
More than your lord's departure weep not. More is   25
    not seen;
Or if it be, 'tis with false Sorrow's eye,
Which for things true weeps things imaginary.
  Queen. It may be so, but yet my inward soul
Persuades me it is otherwise. Howere it be,
I cannot but be sad, so heavy sad   30
As, though on thinking on no thought I think,
Makes me with heavy nothing faint and shrink.

12 **nothing** i.e. the sorrow yet unborn. **something** stressed — ´.
14 **shadows** i.e. false images. 15 **shows** a fairly common plural
form (see also II.3.5, III.3.168, V.3.94). 16 **eye** F; Qq *eyes.* 18
perspectives optical toys of various kinds; stressed ´ — ´.
rightly from the front (also a pun). 20 **Distinguish form** show
distinct shapes or designs. 22 **himself** i.e. King Richard. 23 **Which**
i.e. the collection of apparent griefs. 25 **More than . . . seen**
an alexandrine; hence F *more's.*

Bushy. 'Tis nothing but conceit, my gracious lady.
Queen. 'Tis nothing less. Conceit is still deriv'd
From some forefather grief. Mine is not so,   35
For nothing hath begot my something grief,
Or something hath the nothing that I grieve.
'Tis in reversion that I do possess ;
But what it is, that is not yet known—what
I cannot name. 'Tis nameless woe, I wot.   40

[*Enter Green.*]

Green. God save your majesty ! All well met, gen-
        tlemen.
I hope the king is not yet shipp'd for Ireland.
Queen. Why hop'st thou so? 'Tis better hope he is,
For his designs crave haste, his haste good hope.
Then wherefore dost thou hope he is not shipp'd?   45
Green. That he, our hope, might have retir'd his
        power
And driven into despair an enemy's hope
Who strongly hath set footing in this land.
The banish'd Bullingbrooke repeals himself
And with uplifted arms is safe arriv'd   50
At Ravenspurgh.
Queen.   Now God in heaven forbid !
Green. Ah, madam, 'tis too true ! And that is worse,
The Lord Northumberland, his son young Henry
    Percy,

33 conceit fancy, imagination. 34 nothing less anything but fancy.
35 forefather grief i.e. former grief. 36 nothing no real cause.
something real, actual. 37 nothing the unreal object of grief.
38 'Tis . . . possess N. 46 That demonstrative adjective. 49 repeals himself recalls himself from exile. 50 uplifted i.e. ready to
fight.

The Lords of Ross, Beaumont, and Willoughby,
With all their powerful friends, are fled to him. 55
  Bushy. Why have you not proclaim'd Northumber-
    land
And all the rest revolted faction, traitors?
  Green. We have; whereupon the Earl of Worcester
Hath broken his staff, resign'd his stewardship,
And all the household servants fled with him to Bul-
    lingbrooke. 60
  Queen. So, Green, thou art the midwife to my woe,
And Bullingbrooke my sorrow's dismal heir.
Now hath my soul brought forth her prodigy,
And I, a gasping new-deliver'd mother,
Have woe to woe, sorrow to sorrow, join'd. 65
  Bushy. Despair not, madam.
  Queen.   Who shall hinder me?
I will despair, and be at enmity
With cozening Hope. He is a flatterer,
A parasite, a keeper-back of Death,
Who gently would dissolve the bands of life 70
Which false Hope lingers in extremity.

            [Enter York.]

  Green. Here comes the Duke of York.
  Queen. With signs of war about his aged neck.
O, full of careful business are his looks!

54 **Beaumont** Henry, fifth Baron Beaumont, an unimportant
Yorkshire baron. 57 **all the rest** other Qq, F *the rest of the.* 58 **Earl
of Worcester** Thomas Percy, Northumberland's brother. 59
broken monosyllabic; hence other Qq, F *broke.* 60 **to Bullingbrooke** a separate line in most editions. 62 dismal ill-omened.
63 **prodigy** here a monstrous birth. 71 **Hope lingers** F *hopes
linger.* **lingers** causes to linger. 73 **signs of war** armor. 74 **careful**
anxious.

Uncle, for God's sake, speak comfortable words.   75
    York. Should I do so, I should belie my thoughts.
Comfort's in heaven, and we are on the earth,
Where nothing lives but crosses, cares, and grief.
Your husband, he is gone to save far off
Whilst others come to make him lose at home.   80
Here am I left to underprop his land,
Who, weak with age, cannot support myself.
Now comes the sick hour that his surfeit made;
Now shall he try his friends that flatter'd him.

[Enter a servingman.]

    Servingman. My lord, your son was gone before I
        came.   85
    York. He was? Why, so! Go all which way it will!
The nobles they are fled; the commons they are cold
And will, I fear, revolt on Herford's side.
Sirrah, get thee to Plashie to my sister Gloucester.
Bid her send me presently a thousand pound.   90
Hold, take my ring.
    Servingman. My lord, I had forgot to tell your
        lordship,
Today, as I came by, I called there—
But I shall grieve you to report the rest.
    York. What is't, knave?   95
    Servingman. An hour before I came the duchess
        died.
    York. God for his mercy! What a tide of woes
Comes rushing on this woeful land at once!

76 Should . . . thoughts not in F. 78 crosses troubles, vexations.
83 surfeit i.e. extravagant conduct. 85 son was gone Aumerle
joined Richard in Dublin. 87 The nobles . . . cold an alexandrine. 89 Sirrah . . . Gloucester N. Sirrah a condescending term
of address. Plashie (see I.2.66) N. 97 God for i.e. I pray God for.
48

I know not what to do. I would to God—
So my untruth had not provok'd him to it—   100
The king had cut off my head with my brother's.
What, are there no posts dispatch'd for Ireland?
How shall we do for money for these wars?
Come, sister—cousin, I would say—pray pardon me.
Go, fellow, get thee home, provide some carts   105
And bring away the armor that is there.

                          [*Exit servingman.*]

Gentlemen, will you go muster men?
If I know how or which way to order these affairs
Thus disorderly thrust into my hands,
Never believe me. Both are my kinsmen.   110
T' one is my sovereign, whom both my oath
And duty bids defend; t' other again
Is my kinsman, whom the king hath wrong'd,
Whom conscience and my kinred bids to right.
Well, somewhat we must do. Come, cousin,   115
I'll dispose of you. Gentlemen, go muster up your
          men
And meet me presently at Barkly.
I should to Plashie too,
But time will not permit. All is uneven,
And everything is left at six and seven.   120

                          Exeunt Duke, Queen.

100 **untruth** disloyalty. 101 **brother's** i.e. Gloucester's. 102 **there no posts** F *there postes.* 104 **sister** i.e. the Duchess of Gloucester. 109 **disorderly thrust** so Qq, Ff, but most editions read *thrust disorderly*. 111 **T' one** F *Th' one.* **sovereign** trisyllabic. 112 **bids** singular with the collective subject *oath* and *duty*. **t' other** F *th' other.* 116 **dispose of you** find you a safe place. 117 **presently** at once. **Barkly** Berkeley (pronounced 'Barkly'). 118–19 **I . . . permit** one line in Q, F.

Bushy. The wind sits fair for news to go for Ire-
land,
But none returns. For us to levy power
Proportionable to the enemy is all unpossible.

Green. Besides, our nearness to the king in love
Is near the hate of those love not the king. 125

Bagot. And that is the wavering commons, for their
love
Lies in their purses, and whoso empties them
By so much fills their hearts with deadly hate.

Bushy. Wherein the king stands generally condemn'd.

Bagot. If judgment lie in them, then so do we, 130
Because we ever have been near the king.

Green. Well, I will for refuge straight to Bristow
Castle.
The Earl of Wiltshire is already there.

Bushy. Thither will I with you, for little office
Will the hateful commons perform for us, 135
Except like curs to tear us all to pieces.
Will you go along with us?

Bagot. No, I will to Ireland to his majesty.
Farewell. If heart's presages be not vain,
We three here part that nere shall meet again. 140

Bushy. That's as York thrives to beat back Bullingbrooke.

Green. Alas, poor duke! The task he undertakes
Is numb'ring sands and drinking oceans dry.

---

121 for Ireland F *to Ireland.* 126 that is read 'that's' as F. wavering (disyllabic) fickle. 129 Wherein i.e. in emptying their purses.
130 them i.e. the hearts of the commons. so do we i.e. stand
condemned. 132 I will read 'I'll' (also in l. 138). Bristow N. 134
office service. 135 hateful full of hate.

Where one on his side fights, thousands will fly.
Farewell at once, for once, for all, and ever. 145
  Bushy. Well, we may meet again.
  Bagot.   I fear me, never.
                              [Exeunt.]

SCENE 3

*Enter [Bullingbrooke, the Duke of] Herford,
and Northumberland.*

  Bullingbrooke. How far is it, my lord, to Barkly
    now?
  Northumberland. Believe me, noble lord,
I am a stranger here in Gloucestershire.
These high wild hills and rough uneven ways
Draws out our miles and makes them wearisome, 5
And yet your fair discourse hath been as sugar,
Making the hard way sweet and delectable.
But I bethink me what a weary way
From Ravenspurgh to Cotshall will be found
In Ross and Willoughby, wanting your company, 10
Which, I protest, hath very much beguil'd
The tediousness and process of my travel.
But theirs is sweet'ned with the hope to have
The present benefit which I possess,
And hope to joy is little less in joy 15
Than hope enjoy'd. By this the weary lords
Shall make their way seem short as mine hath done
By sight of what I have, your noble company.

5 Draws see II.2.15. 6 your F *our.* 7 delectable stressed $\underline{\prime} - \underline{\smallsmile}$
—. 9 Cotshall Cotswold (local pronunciation probably 'Cots'l'). 10 In in the case of. 12 **tediousness and process** hendiadys. 15 **to joy** to enjoy.

Bullingbrooke. Of much less value is my company
Than your good words. But who comes here?   20

Enter Harry Percy.

Northumberland. It is my son, young Harry Percy,
Sent from my brother Worcester, whencesoever.
Harry, how fares your uncle?

Percy. I had thought, my lord, to have learn'd his
health of you.

Northumberland. Why, is he not with the queen?   25

Percy. No, my good lord. He hath forsook the
court,
Broken his staff of office, and dispers'd
The household of the king.

Northumberland.   What was his reason?
He was not so resolv'd when last we spake togither.

Percy. Because your lordship was proclaim'd trai-
tor.   30
But he, my lord, is gone to Ravenspurgh
To offer service to the Duke of Herford,
And sent me over by Barkly to discover
What power the Duke of York had levied there,
Then with directions to repair to Ravenspurgh.   35

Northumberland. Have you forgot the Duke of
Herford, boy?

Percy. No, my good lord, for that is not forgot
Which nere I did remember. To my knowledge,
I never in my life did look on him.

Northumberland. Then learn to know him now. This
is the duke.   40

24 I had read 'I'd.' to have read 't' have.' 28–9 What . . . resolv'd F's lineation; one line in Q. 33 over read 'o'er.' 36 Herford,
boy F; Q *Herefords boy.*

52

Percy. My gracious lord, I tender you my service,
Such as it is, being tender, raw, and young—
Which elder days shall ripen and confirm
To more approved service and desert.
  Bullingbrooke. I thank thee, gentle Percy, and be
    sure   45
I count myself in nothing else so happy
As in a soul rememb'ring my good friends.
And as my fortune ripens with thy love,
It shall be still thy true love's recompense.   49
My heart this covenant makes, my hand thus seals it.
  Northumberland. How far is it to Barkly? And
    what stir
Keeps good old York there with his men of war?
  Percy. There stands the castle by yon tuft of trees,
Mann'd with three hundred men, as I have heard,
And in it are the Lords of York, Barkly, and Sey-
    mer—   55
None else of name and noble estimate.

[*Enter Ross and Willoughby.*]

  Northumberland. Here come the Lords of Ross and
    Willoughby,
Bloody with spurring, fiery red with haste.
  Bullingbrooke. Welcome, my lords. I wot your love
    pursues
A banish'd traitor. All my treasury   60
Is yet but unfelt thanks, which more enrich'd

41–2 tender, tender both puns. **44 approved** tested. **50 covenant**
disyllabic. **55 Barkly** Thomas, Lord Berkeley. **Seymer** Richard,
Lord Seymour (pronounced 'Seemer'); other Qq, F *Seymor.* **56
estimate** repute, estimation. **61 unfelt** of no tangible worth.
which i.e. treasury.

Shall be your love and labor's recompense.

Ross. Your presence makes us rich, most noble lord.

Willoughby. And far surmounts our labor to attain it.

Bullingbrooke. Evermore thanks, the exchequer of the poor,   65

Which, till my infant fortune comes to years,

Stands for my bounty. But who comes here?

[*Enter Barkly.*]

Northumberland. It is my Lord of Barkly, as I guess.

Barkly. My Lord of Herford, my message is to you.

Bullingbrooke. My lord, my answer is—to Lancaster,   70

And I am come to seek that name in England,

And I must find that title in your tongue

Before I make reply to aught you say.

Barkly. Mistake me not, my lord. 'Tis not my meaning

To rase one title of your honor out.   75

To you, my lord, I come, what lord you will,

From the most gracious regent of this land,

The Duke of York, to know what pricks you on

To take advantage of the absent time   79

And fright our native peace with self-borne arms.

[*Enter York, attended.*]

65 the exchequer read 'th' exchequer.' **70 my answer . . . Lancaster** N. **72 title** a possible pun ('title' and 'tittle' were probably pronounced alike). **76 what lord you will** whatever title you prefer. **77 gracious regent** of F *glorious of.* **79 absent time** i.e. time of Richard's absence. **80 self-borne** borne for himself (not the king) N.

Bullingbrooke. I shall not need transport my words
    by you.
Here comes his grace in person. My noble uncle!
                          [*Kneels.*]
   York. Show me thy humble heart, and not thy knee,
Whose duty is deceivable and false.
   Bullingbrooke. My gracious uncle! 85
   York. Tut, tut! Grace me no grace, nor uncle me
    no uncle.
I am no traitor's uncle, and that word 'grace'
In an ungracious mouth is but profane.
Why have those banish'd and forbidden legs
Dar'd once to touch a dust of England's ground? 90
But then more 'why?' Why have they dar'd to march
So many miles upon her peaceful bosom,
Frighting her pale-fac'd villages with war
And ostentation of despised arms?
Com'st thou because the anointed king is hence? 95
Why, foolish boy, the king is left behind,
And in my loyal bosom lies his power.
Were I but now the lord of such hot youth
As when brave Gaunt thy father and myself 99
Rescued the Black Prince, that young Mars of men,
From forth the ranks of many thousand French,
O, then how quickly should this arm of mine,

---

84 duty reverence. 86 **Grace me no grace** call me not gracious.
no uncle not in F. 90 **a dust** a grain of dust. 91 **But then more**
'why?' Q2–4 *But more than why;* Q5, F *But more then why.* **more**
'why?' i.e. more questions to ask. 93 **pale-fac'd** faces made pale
from fright; proleptic. 95 **anointed** read 'th' anointed'; see I.2.38.
hence i.e. in Ireland. 98 **the** F; not in Qq. 99–101 **As when . . .**
French no historical basis is known for this.

Now prisoner to the palsy, chastise thee
And minister correction to thy fault!
 Bullingbrooke. My gracious uncle, let me know my
  fault.   105
On what condition stands it and wherein?
 York. Even in condition of the worst degree,
In gross rebellion and detested treason.
Thou art a banish'd man and here art come,
Before the expiration of thy time,   110
In braving arms against thy sovereign.
 Bullingbrooke. As I was banish'd, I was banish'd
  Herford,
But as I come, I come for Lancaster.
And, noble uncle, I beseech your grace
Look on my wrongs with an indifferent eye.   115
You are my father, for methinks in you
I see old Gaunt alive. O, then, my father,
Will you permit that I shall stand condemn'd
A wandering vagabond, my rights and royalties
Pluck'd from my arms perforce, and given away 120
To upstart unthrifts? Wherefore was I born?
If that my cousin king be king in England,
It must be granted I am Duke of Lancaster.
You have a son, Aumerle, my noble cousin.
Had you first died, and he bin thus trod down, 125
He should have found his uncle Gaunt a father
To rouse his wrongs and chase them to the bay.
I am denied to sue my livery here,

103 prisoner disyllabic. palsy paralysis. chastise stressed ⏑ —.
106 On what . . . wherein N. 111 braving defiant. 113 for **Lancaster** N. 115 **indifferent** impartial. 119 wandering, royalties both
disyllabic. 122 **in England** other Qq, F *of England*. 124 **cousin** F
Kinsman. 127 **chase . . . bay** put them at bay (a hunting expression).

And yet my letters-patents give me leave.
My father's goods are all distrain'd and sold, 130
And these, and all, are all amiss employ'd.
What would you have me do? I am a subject,
And I challenge law. Attorneys are denied me,
And therefore personally I lay my claim
To my inheritance of free descent. 135
  Northumberland. The noble duke hath been too
    much abus'd.
  Ross. It stands your grace upon to do him right.
  Willoughby. Base men by his endowments are made
    great.
  York. My lords of England, let me tell you this:
I have had feeling of my cousin's wrongs, 140
And labor'd all I could to do him right,
But in this kind to come, in braving arms,
Be his own carver and cut out his way
To find out right with wrong—it may not be.
And you that do abet him in this kind 145
Cherish rebellion and are rebels all.
  Northumberland. The noble duke hath sworn his
    coming is
But for his own, and for the right of that
We all have strongly sworn to give him aid, 149
And let him never see joy that breaks that oath!
  York. Well, well, I see the issue of these arms.
I cannot mend it, I must needs confess,

---

129 letters-patents see II.1.202 N. 130 distrain'd seized by writ.
133 I not in F. challenge law claim my legal rights. 135 free
direct, legitimate. 137 stands your grace upon is your grace's
duty. 138 Base low in rank. endowments revenues from lands.
141 labor'd all I could i.e. by protesting to Richard. 142 kind
i.e. way of acting. 144 wrong F *Wrongs.* 150 never read 'ne'er.'

Because my power is weak and all ill left.
But if I could, by Him that gave me life
I would attach you all and make you stoop   155
Unto the sovereign mercy of the king.
But since I cannot, be it known unto you
I do remain as neuter. So fare you well—
Unless you please to enter in the castle
And there repose you for this night.   160
    Bullingbrooke. An offer, uncle, that we will accept.
But we must win your grace to go with us
To Bristow Castle, which they say is held
By Bushy, Bagot, and their complices,
The caterpillars of the commonwealth,   165
Which I have sworn to weed and pluck away.
    York. It may be I will go with you. But yet I'll
        pause,
For I am loath to break our country's laws.
Nor friends nor foes, to me welcome you are.   169
Things past redress are now with me past care.
                                    Exeunt.

SCENE 4

Enter the Earl of Salisbury and a Welsh captain.

Captain. My Lord of Salisbury, we have stay'd ten
        days
And hardly kept our countrymen together,
And yet we hear no tidings from the king.
Therefore we will disperse ourselves. Farewell.

---

153 ill left badly provided for. 155 attach arrest. 165 caterpillars
i.e. greedy parasites. 169 welcome stressed — $\stackrel{\prime}{-}$. 1 Captain F;
Qq *Welch*[*man*]. Salisbury disyllabic. 2 hardly with difficulty.

Salisbury. Stay yet another day, thou trusty
    Welshman.   5
The king reposeth all his confidence in thee.
  Captain. 'Tis thought the king is dead. We will
    not stay.
The bay trees in our country are all wither'd,
And meteors fright the fixed stars of heaven.
The pale-fac'd moon looks bloody on the earth,   10
And lean-look'd prophets whisper fearful change.
Rich men look sad and ruffians dance and leap,
The one in fear to lose what they enjoy,
The other to enjoy by rage and war.
These signs forerun the death or fall of kings.   15
Farewell. Our countrymen are gone and fled,
As well assur'd Richard their king is dead.   [*Exit.*]
  Salisbury. Ah, Richard! With the eyes of heavy
    mind
I see thy glory like a shooting star
Fall to the base earth from the firmament.   20
Thy sun sets weeping in the lowly west,
Witnessing storms to come, woe, and unrest.
Thy friends are fled to wait upon thy foes,
And crossly to thy good all fortune goes.   [*Exit.*]

6 The king . . . thee an alexandrine. 8 are all other Qq, F *all
are.* 11 lean-look'd i.e. lean-faced. 14 to in hope to. rage tumult.
15 or fall not in other Qq, F. 18 the not in other Qq, F. 21 weeping pathetic fallacy; also 'watery.' 22 Witnessing portending.
24 crossly adversely.

Act III

SCENE 1

*Enter [Bullingbrooke,] the Duke of Herford,
York, Northumberland, [Ross, Percy, Willoughby, with] Bushy and Green prisoners.*

Bullingbrooke. Bring forth these men.
Bushy and Green, I will not vex your souls—
Since presently your souls must part your bodies—
With too much urging your pernicious lives,
For 'twere no charity. Yet, to wash your blood   5
From off my hands, here in the view of men
I will unfold some causes of your deaths.
You have misled a prince, a royal king,
A happy gentleman in blood and lineaments,
By you unhappied and disfigur'd clean.   10
You have in manner with your sinful hours
Made a divorce betwixt his queen and him,
Broke the possession of a royal bed
And stain'd the beauty of a fair queen's cheeks   14
With tears drawn from her eyes by your foul wrongs.
Myself, a prince by fortune of my birth,
Near to the king in blood, and near in love
Till you did make him misinterpret me,
Have stoop'd my neck under your injuries

5 charity (disyllabic) kindness. 9 happy fortunate. 10 clean com-
pletely. 11 in manner in a way. sinful hours i.e. of riotous living.
13 Broke . . . bed mentioned only in Holinshed. Broke inter-
rupted.

60

And sigh'd my English breath in foreign clouds,   20
Eating the bitter bread of banishment,
Whilst you have fed upon my signories,
Dispark'd my parks and fell'd my forest woods,
From my own windows torn my household coat,
Ras'd out my imprese, leaving me no sign,   25
Save men's opinions and my living blood,
To show the world I am a gentleman.
This and much more, much more than twice all this,
Condemns you to the death. See them deliver'd over
To execution and the hand of death.   30
   Bushy. More welcome is the stroke of death to me
Than Bullingbrooke to England. Lords, farewell.
   Green. My comfort is that heaven will take our
      souls
And plague injustice with the pains of hell.
   Bullingbrooke. My Lord Northumberland, see
      them dispatch'd.   35
         [*Exeunt Northumberland and others,
                  with the prisoners.*]

Uncle, you say the queen is at your house.
For God's sake, fairly let her be entreated.
Tell her I send to her my kind commends.
Take special care my greetings be deliver'd.
   York. A gentleman of mine I have dispatch'd   40
With letters of your love to her at large.
   Bullingbrooke. Thanks, gentle uncle. Come, lords,
      away,

20 in into. 22 signories estates, manors. 23 **Dispark'd** reduced to a
common (a legal term). 24 household coat coat of arms painted
on the glass. 25 imprese crest or heraldic device. 26 my living
blood myself while still living. 32 Lords, farewell not in F. 36
your house i.e. Langley. 37 entreated treated. 41 at large at
great length.

To fight with Glendor and his complices.
Awhile to work, and after holiday.   *Exeunt.*

SCENE 2

*[Drums. Flourish and colors.] Enter the King,
Aumerle, [the Bishop of] Carlisle [, and soldiers].*

King Richard. Barkloughly Castle call they this
      at hand?
Aumerle. Yea, my lord. How brooks your grace
      the air
After your late tossing on the breaking seas?
King Richard. Needs must I like it well. I weep for
      joy
To stand upon my kingdom once again.   5
Dear earth, I do salute thee with my hand,
Though rebels wound thee with their horses' hoofs.
As a long-parted mother with her child
Plays fondly with her tears and smiles in meeting,
So weeping, smiling, greet I thee my earth,   10
And do thee favors with my royal hands.
Feed not thy sovereign's foe, my gentle earth,
Nor with thy sweets comfort his ravenous sense;
But let thy spiders that suck up thy venom,
And heavy-gaited toads, lie in their way,   15
Doing annoyance to the treacherous feet
Which with usurping steps do trample thee.
Yield stinging nettles to mine enemies,

43 Glendor Glendower; F *Glendoure* N. 1 Barkloughly Castle N.
2 brooks endures, and also enjoys. 8 with from. 11 favors F *fauor.*
13 comfort stressed — $\angle$. 15 heavy-gaited slow-paced. toads
thought to be poisonous. 16 annoyance injury.

And when they from thy bosom pluck a flower,
Guard it, I pray thee, with a lurking adder   20
Whose double tongue may with a mortal touch
Throw death upon thy sovereign's enemies.
Mock not my senseless conjuration, lords.
This earth shall have a feeling, and these stones
Prove armed soldiers ere her native king   25
Shall falter under foul rebellion's arms.
  Carlisle. Fear not, my lord. That power that made
    you king
Hath power to keep you king in spite of all.
The means that heavens yield must be embrac'd,
And not neglected. Else if heaven would   30
And we will not, heaven's offer we refuse,
The proffer'd means of succors and redress.
  Aumerle. He means, my lord, that we are too remiss
Whilst Bullingbrooke, through our security,   34
Grows strong and great in substance and in power.
  King Richard. Discomfortable cousin! Know'st
    thou not
That when the searching eye of heaven is hid
Behind the globe that lights the lower world,
Then thieves and robbers range abroad unseen
In murthers and in outrage boldly here;   40
But when from under this terrestrial ball
He fires the proud tops of the eastern pines

21 **double** forked N. **mortal** fatal. 22 **Throw** spit, inflict. 23 **sense-less conjuration** conjuring of things that lack feeling. 25 **native** lawful, natural. 29–32 **The means . . . redress** N. 34 **security** overconfidence, carelessness. 35 **power** F *friends;* compare II.3.34. 36 **Discomfortable** discouraging. 37 **eye of heaven** the sun N. 38 **that** antecedent: *eye of heaven.* **lower world** i.e. the antip-odes. 40 **murthers** murders. **boldly** Q *bouldy;* other Qq *bloudy;* F *bloody.* 42 **proud** lofty.

And darts his light through every guilty hole,
Then murthers, treasons, and detested sins,
The cloak of night being pluck'd from off their
    backs,   45
Stand bare and naked, trembling at themselves?
So when this thief, this traitor, Bullingbrooke,
Who all this while hath revel'd in the night
Whilst we were wand'ring with the antipodes,
Shall see us rising in our throne, the east,   50
His treasons will sit blushing in his face,
Not able to endure the sight of day,
But self-affrighted tremble at his sin.
Not all the water in the rough rude sea
Can wash the balm off from an anointed king.   55
The breath of worldly men cannot depose
The deputy elected by the Lord.
For every man that Bullingbrooke hath press'd
To lift shrewd steel against our golden crown,
God for his Richard hath in heavenly pay   60
A glorious angel. Then, if angels fight,
Weak men must fall, for heaven still guards the
    right.

Enter Salisbury.

Welcome, my lord. How far off lies your power?
  Salisbury. Nor near nor farther off, my gracious
    lord,   64
Than this weak arm. Discomfort guides my tongue
And bids me speak of nothing but despair.

---

43 light F *Lightning.* guilty hole where the guilty hide. 49 Whilst
. . . antipodes not in F. the antipodes read 'th' antipodes';
people on the opposite side of the earth. 55 balm oil used to
anoint a king. off . . . anointed N. 56 worldly mortal. 59 shrewd
sharp and malicious. 64 near nearer.

One day too late, I fear me, noble lord,
Hath clouded all thy happy days on earth.
O, call back yesterday, bid time return,   69
And thou shalt have twelve thousand fighting men!
Today, today, unhappy day, too late,
Overthrows thy joys, friends, fortune, and thy
    state.
For all the Welshmen, hearing thou wert dead,
Are gone to Bullingbrooke, dispers'd, and fled.
    Aumerle. Comfort, my liege. Why looks your grace
        so pale?   75
    King Richard. But now the blood of twenty thou-
        sand men
    Did triumph in my face, and they are fled.
And till so much blood thither come again,
    Have I not reason to look pale and dead?
All souls that will be safe, fly from my side,   80
For time hath set a blot upon my pride.
    Aumerle. Comfort, my liege. Remember who you
        are.
    King Richard. I had forgot myself. Am I not king?
Awake, thou coward majesty! Thou sleep'st.
Is not the king's name twenty thousand names?   85
Arm, arm, my name! A puny subject strikes
At thy great glory. Look not to the ground,
Ye favorites of a king. Are we not high?
High be our thoughts. I know my uncle York
Hath power enough to serve our turn. But who
    comes here?   90

67 **One day too late** i.e. his arrival a day late. 70 **twelve** forty,
according to Holinshed. 72 **Overthrows** read 'o'erthrows'; F
Orethrowes. 76–9 **But now . . . dead** a quatrain. 76 **But** just.
twenty indefinite but large number. 84 **coward** F *sluggard.* 85
twenty F *fortie.*

Enter Scroop.

Scroop. More health and happiness betide my liege
Than can my care-tun'd tongue deliver him!
   King Richard. Mine ear is open and my heart pre-
     par'd.
The worst is wordly loss thou canst unfold.
Say, is my kingdom lost? Why, 'twas my care, 95
And what loss is it to be rid of care?
Strives Bullingbrooke to be as great as we?
Greater he shall not be. If he serve God,
We'll serve Him too and be his fellow so.
Revolt our subjects? That we cannot mend. 100
They break their faith to God as well as us.
Cry woe, destruction, ruin, and decay;
The worst is death, and death will have his day.
   Scroop. Glad am I that your highness is so arm'd
To bear the tidings of calamity. 105
Like an unseasonable stormy day
Which makes the silver rivers drown their shores
As if the world were all dissolv'd to tears,
So high above his limits swells the rage
Of Bullingbrooke, covering your fearful land 110
With hard bright steel and hearts harder than steel.
Whitebeards have arm'd their thin and hairless
     scalps
Against thy majesty. Boys with women's voices
Strive to speak big and clap their female joints

SD **Scroop** Sir Stephen Scroop, Wiltshire's elder brother. 91
More . . . betide may more . . . befall. 99 be his fellow so
thus be Bolingbroke's equal. 102 **destruction, ruin, and decay**
synonyms. **and decay** F *Losse, Decay.* 109 his its. 110 **covering**
disyllabic. 112 **Whitebeards** old men. **arm'd** i.e. with helmets.
114 **big** deeply (like men). **female** i.e. weak.

In stiff unwieldy arms against thy crown.   115
Thy very beadsmen learn to bend their bows
Of double-fatal yew against thy state.
Yea, distaff-women manage rusty bills
Against thy seat. Both young and old rebel,
And all goes worse than I have power to tell.   120
  King Richard. Too well, too well thou tell'st a tale
    so ill.
Where is the Earl of Wiltshire? Where is Bagot?
What is become of Bushy? Where is Green?—
That they have let the dangerous enemy
Measure our confines with such peaceful steps?   125
If we prevail, their heads shall pay for it.
I warrant they have made peace with Bullingbrooke.
  Scroop. Peace have they made with him indeed, my
    lord.
  King Richard. O villains, vipers, damn'd without
    redemption!
Dogs, easily won to fawn on any man!   130
Snakes, in my heart-blood warm'd, that sting my
    heart!
Three Judases, each one thrice worse than Judas!
Would they make peace? Terrible hell
Make war upon their spotted souls for this!   134
  Scroop. Sweet love, I see, changing his property,
Turns to the sourest and most deadly hate.
Again uncurse their souls. Their peace is made

---

115 In into. 116 beadsmen almsmen, old pensioners. 117 double
both as poisonous berries and as deadly bows. state royalty.
118 distaff-women women who should only spin. bills a pike—
battle-ax combination. 119 seat throne. 122 Where is Bagot N.
125 Measure traverse. peaceful unresisted. 127 they have read
'they've.' 130 easily disyllabic. 134 Make war . . . this N.
spotted wicked (not spotless). 135 his property its nature.

With heads and not with hands. Those whom you
    curse
Have felt the worst of death's destroying wound
And lie full low, grav'd in the hollow ground.   140
   Aumerle. Is Bushy, Green, and the Earl of Wilt-
    shire dead?
   Scroop. Ay, all of them at Bristow lost their heads.
   Aumerle. Where is the duke my father with his
    power?
   King Richard. No matter where. Of comfort no man
    speak.
Let's talk of graves, of worms, and epitaphs,   145
Make dust our paper, and with rainy eyes
Write sorrow on the bosom of the earth.
Let's choose executors and talk of wills.
And yet not so, for what can we bequeath
Save our deposed bodies to the ground?   150
Our lands, our lives, and all are Bullingbrooke's,
And nothing can we call our own but death
And that small model of the barren earth
Which serves as paste and cover to our bones.
For God's sake, let us sit upon the ground   155
And tell sad stories of the death of kings—
How some have been depos'd, some slain in war,
Some haunted by the ghosts they have depos'd,
Some poison'd by their wives, some sleeping kill'd,
All murther'd. For within the hollow crown   160
That rounds the mortal temples of a king
Keeps Death his court, and there the antic sits,

138 **heads** see l. 142. **hands** i.e. hands raised submissively. 139
wound F *hand*. 153 **model . . . earth** grave mound, or earthly
body. 154 **paste and cover** like top crust on a pie; hendiadys.
158 **ghosts they** ghosts of those whom they. 162 **antic** Death as a
grinning buffoon.

Scoffing his state and grinning at his pomp,
Allowing him a breath, a little scene,
To monarchize, be fear'd, and kill with looks,   165
Infusing him with self and vain conceit,
As if this flesh which walls about our life
Were brass impregnable, and humor'd thus
Comes at the last and with a little pin   169
Bores through his castle wall, and farewell king!
Cover your heads and mock not flesh and blood
With solemn reverence. Throw away respect,
Tradition, form, and ceremonious duty,
For you have but mistook me all this while.
I live with bread like you, feel want,   175
Taste grief, need friends. Subjected thus,
How can you say to me I am a king?
  Carlisle. My lord, wise men nere sit and wail their
        woes,
But presently prevent the ways to wail.
To fear the foe, since fear oppresseth strength,   180
Gives in your weakness strength unto your foe,
And so your follies fight against yourself.
Fear, and be slain—no worse can come to fight.
And fight and die is death destroying death,
Where fearing dying pays death servile breath.   185
  Aumerle. My father hath a power. Inquire of him,

163 Scoffing sometimes transitive. 166 self and vain conceit vain
self-conceit. 168 humor'd thus his humor satisfied (either Death's
or the king's or both). 169 Comes i.e. Death comes. 170 his castle
wall i.e. his body. wall other Qq, F *Walls*. 171 Cover your heads
even though in the royal presence. 178 sit . . . woes F *waile
their present woes*. 179 presently . . . wail i.e. promptly cut off
the causes of grief. 182 And . . . yourself not in F. 183 to fight
in fighting. 185 Where whereas. 186 My father i.e. York. power
army. of about.

And learn to make a body of a limb.
   King Richard. Thou chid'st me well. Proud Bulling-
      brooke, I come
To change blows with thee for our day of doom.
This ague fit of fear is overblown.   190
An easy task it is to win our own.
Say, Scroop, where lies our uncle with his power?
Speak sweetly, man, although thy looks be sour.
   Scroop. Men judge by the complexion of the sky
    The state and inclination of the day.   195
So may you by my dull and heavy eye:
   My tongue hath but a heavier tale to say.
I play the torturer, by small and small
To lengthen out the worst that must be spoken.
Your uncle York is join'd with Bullingbrooke,   200
And all your northern castles yielded up,
And all your southern gentlemen in arms
Upon his party.
   King Richard.   Thou hast said enough.
[*To Aumerle.*] Beshrew thee, cousin, which didst lead
   me forth
Of that sweet way I was in to despair!   205
What say you now? What comfort have we now?
By heaven, I'll hate him everlastingly
That bids me be of comfort any more.
Go to Flint Castle. There I'll pine away.
A king, woe's slave, shall kingly woe obey.   210

---

187 to make . . . limb i.e. to make the best of what one has.
189 for . . . doom i.e. to see which one dies. 194–7 Men judge
. . . say a quatrain. 199 lengthen out delay, defer; allusion to
torture on the rack. 203 Upon his party on Bolingbroke's side.
party F *Faction.* 204 Beshrew ill luck take (a mild curse). 205 Of
from. 209 Flint Castle near Chester, in Wales.

That power I have, discharge, and let them go
To ear the land that hath some hope to grow,
For I have none. Let no man speak again
To alter this, for counsel is but vain.   214
    Aumerle. My liege, one word.
    King Richard.   He does me double wrong
That wounds me with the flatteries of his tongue.
Discharge my followers. Let them hence away,
From Richard's night to Bullingbrooke's fair day.
                                    [*Exeunt.*]

SCENE 3

Enter [*with drum and colors*] *Bullingbrooke,
York, Northumberland* [*, attendants, and soldiers.*

    Bullingbrooke. So that by this intelligence we learn
The Welshmen are dispers'd, and Salisbury
Is gone to meet the king, who lately landed
With some few private friends upon this coast.
    Northumberland. The news is very fair and good,
        my lord.   5
Richard not far from hence hath hid his head.
    York. It would beseem the Lord Northumberland
To say 'King Richard.' Alack the heavy day
When such a sacred king should hide his head!
    Northumberland. Your grace mistakes. Only to be
        brief   10
Left I his title out.
    York.   The time hath bin,
Would you have been so brief with him, he would

212 ear plow. 10 mistakes perhaps to be read 'mistaketh,' to
regularize the line. 11–13 The time . . . shorten you F's lineation
(Q ends l. 12 with *him*).

Have bin so brief with you to shorten you,
For taking so the head, your whole head's length.
Bullingbrooke. Mistake not, uncle, further than
you should. 15
York. Take not, good cousin, further than you
should,
Lest you mistake. The heavens are over our heads.
Bullingbrooke. I know it, uncle, and oppose not
myself
Against their will. But who comes here? 19

Enter Percy.

Welcome, Harry. What, will not this castle yield?
Percy. The castle royally is mann'd, my lord,
Against thy entrance.
Bullingbrooke. Royally!
Why, it contains no king?
Percy. Yes, my good lord,
It doth contain a king. King Richard lies 25
Within the limits of yon lime and stone.
And with him are the Lord Aumerle, Lord Salisbury,
Sir Stephen Scroop, besides a clergyman
Of holy reverence—who, I cannot learn.
Northumberland. O, belike it is the Bishop of
Carlisle. 30
Bullingbrooke. Noble lords,
Go to the rude ribs of that ancient castle.

13 brief unceremonious. with you F; not in Qq. to shorten as to
shorten. 14 For . . . head N. 15 Mistake not i.e. do not take
amiss Northumberland's words. 16 cousin nephew. 17 mistake
both 'misjudge' and 'mis-take' (a quibble). mistake. The Qq, F
mistake the. heavens monosyllabic here and elsewhere. over read
'o'er'; F *ore.* 25 lies dwells. 27 are not in other Qq, F. 31 lords
Qq; F *lord.* 32 rude ribs i.e. rough walls.

Through brazen trumpet send the breath of parle
Into his ruin'd ears, and thus deliver:
Henry Bullingbrooke   35
On both his knees doth kiss King Richard's hand
And sends allegiance and true faith of heart
To his most royal person, hither come
Even at his feet to lay my arms and power,
Provided that my banishment repeal'd   40
And lands restor'd again be freely granted.
If not, I'll use the advantage of my power
And lay the summer's dust with showers of blood
Rain'd from the wounds of slaughter'd Englishmen.
The which, how far off from the mind of Bulling-
          brooke   45
It is, such crimson tempest should bedrench
The fresh green lap of fair King Richard's land,
My stooping duty tenderly shall show.
Go signify as much while here we march
Upon the grassy carpet of this plain.   50
Let's march without the noise of threat'ning drum,
That from this castle's totter'd battlements
Our fair appointments may be well perus'd.
Methinks King Richard and myself should meet
With no less terror than the elements   55

34 **his ruin'd ears** i.e. its battered windows. 35-6 **Henry . . .
hand** one line in Qq. 38 **most** not in F. 39 **Even** read 'e'en.' **my** N.
40-1 **Provided . . . granted** N. 42 **the advantage** read 'th' advantage.' 43 **showers** monosyllabic. 45 **The which** antecedent:
the whole threat (ll. 42–4). **how** however. 48 **stooping** reverential.
52 **totter'd** variant spelling of 'tattered.' 53 **fair appointments**
splendid and terrible arms and armor. **perus'd** viewed. 55-7
elements . . . heaven an old explanation for thunder.

Of fire and water when their thund'ring shock
At meeting tears the cloudy cheeks of heaven.
Be he the fire, I'll be the yielding water.
The rage be his, whilst on the earth I rain
My waters—on the earth, and not on him.   60
March on, and mark King Richard how he looks.

[*Parle without, and answer within; then a flourish.
Enter, on the walls, King Richard, the Bishop of
Carlisle, Aumerle, Scroop, Salisbury.*]

See, see, King Richard doth himself appear,
As doth the blushing discontented sun
From out the fiery portal of the east
When he perceives the envious clouds are bent   65
To dim his glory and to stain the track
Of his bright passage to the occident.
  York. Yet looks he like a king. Behold his eye,
As bright as is the eagle's, lightens forth
Controlling majesty. Alack, alack, for woe,   70
That any harm should stain so fair a show!
  King Richard. [*To Northumberland.*] We are
    amaz'd, and thus long have we stood
To watch the fearful bending of thy knee,
Because we thought ourself thy lawful king.
And if we be, how dare thy joints forget   75
To pay their awful duty to our presence?
If we be not, show us the hand of God
That hath dismiss'd us from our stewardship;
For well we know no hand of blood and bone
Can gripe the sacred handle of our scepter   80
Unless he do profane, steal, or usurp.

56 shock F *smoake*. SD Parle . . . Salisbury N. 66 track F *tract*.
69–70 lightens . . . majesty flashes with imperious majesty. 72
amaz'd stunned, and in a maze. 73 fearful timorous.

And though you think that all, as you have done,
Have torn their souls by turning them from us,
And we are barren and bereft of friends,
Yet know my master, God omnipotent,   85
Is mustering in his clouds on our behalf
Armies of pestilence; and they shall strike
Your children yet unborn and unbegot
That lift your vassal hands against my head
And threat the glory of my precious crown.   90
Tell Bullingbrooke—for yon methinks he stands—
That every stride he makes upon my land
Is dangerous treason. He is come to open
The purple testament of bleeding war.
But ere the crown he looks for live in peace,   95
Ten thousand bloody crowns of mother's sons
Shall ill become the flower of England's face,
Change the complexion of her maid-pale peace
To scarlet indignation, and bedew
Her pastors' grass with faithful English blood.   100
  Northumberland. The King of Heaven forbid our
       lord the king
Should so with civil and uncivil arms
Be rush'd upon! Thy thrice-noble cousin
Harry Bullingbrooke doth humbly kiss thy hand.
And by the honorable tomb he swears   105
That stands upon your royal grandsire's bones,

86 **mustering** disyllabic. 89 **That** implied antecedent: 'you' (in
your of l. 88). 93–4 **He is . . . war** N. 93 **open** F *ope*. 95–100
But ere . . . blood a prophecy of the Wars of the Roses. 97 **ill
. . . face** i.e. disfigure the beauty of the land's surface. 100
pastors' pastures' (the words were pronounced alike). 102 **civil
and uncivil** domestic and barbarous. 103 **thrice-noble** N. 106
grandsire's Edward III's.

And by the royalties of both your bloods—
Currents that spring from one most gracious head—
And by the buried hand of warlike Gaunt,
And by worth and honor of himself,   110
Comprising all that may be sworn or said,
His coming hither hath no further scope
Than for his lineal royalties, and to beg
Enfranchisement immediate on his knees.
Which on thy royal party granted once,   115
His glittering arms he will commend to rust,
His barbed steeds to stables, and his heart
To faithful service of your majesty.
This swears he, as he is a prince, is just.
And as I am a gentleman, I credit him.   120

King Richard. Northumberland, say thus the king
        returns:
His noble cousin is right welcome hither,
And all the number of his fair demands
Shall be accomplish'd without contradiction.
With all the gracious utterance thou hast,   125
Speak to his gentle hearing kind commends.
[*To Aumerle.*] We do debase ourselves, cousin, do
        we not,
To look so poorly and to speak so fair?
Shall we call back Northumberland and send
Defiance to the traitor, and so die?   130

Aumerle. No, good my lord, let's fight with gentle
        words

---

107 **royalties** royalty. 113 **royalties** disyllabic. 114 **Enfranchisement** restoration of rights, i.e. freedom. **immediate** trisyllabic.
115 **party** side, part. 116 **glittering** disyllabic. **commend** deliver
up. 117 **barbed** armored. 119 **is a prince, is just** N. just true.
121 **returns** replies. 123 **demands** requests. 127 **ourselves** F *our
selfe.*

Till time lend friends, and friends their helpful
  swords.
   King Richard. O God, O God, that ere this tongue
  of mine
That laid the sentence of dread banishment
On yon proud man, should take it off again   135
With words of sooth! O that I were as great
As is my grief, or lesser than my name!
Or that I could forget what I have been!
Or not remember what I must be now!
Swell'st thou, proud heart? I'll give thee scope to
  beat,   140
Since foes have scope to beat both thee and me.
   Aumerle. Northumberland comes back from Bull-
  ingbrooke.
   King Richard. What must the king do now? Must
  he submit?
The king shall do it. Must he be depos'd?
The king shall be contented. Must he lose   145
The name of king? A God's name, let it go!
I'll give my jewels for a set of beads,
My gorgeous palace for a hermitage,
My gay apparel for an almsman's gown,
My figur'd goblets for a dish of wood,   150
My scepter for a palmer's walking staff,
My subjects for a pair of carved saints,
And my large kingdom for a little grave,
A little little grave, an obscure grave.
Or I'll be buried in the king's highway,   **155**
Some way of common trade, where subjects' **feet**
May hourly trample on their sovereign's head;

136 sooth flattery. **137 name** title. **146 A** in. **147 set of beads**
rosary. **150 figur'd** ornamented. **154 obscure** stressed ⏑ —. **156**
trade traffic.

For on my heart they tread now whilst I live,
And buried once, why not upon my head?   159
Aumerle, thou weep'st, my tender-hearted cousin.
We'll make foul weather with despised tears;
Our sighs and they shall lodge the summer corn
And make a dearth in this revolting land.
Or shall we play the wantons with our woes   164
And make some pretty match with shedding tears?
As thus—to drop them still upon one place
Till they have fretted us a pair of graves
Within the earth, and therein laid—there lies
Two kinsmen digg'd their graves with weeping eyes.
Would not this ill do well? Well, well, I see   170
I talk but idly, and you laugh at me.
Most mighty prince, my Lord Northumberland,
What says King Bullingbrooke? Will his majesty
Give Richard leave to live till Richard die?
You make a leg, and Bullingbrooke says aye.   175
  Northumberland. My lord, in the base court he doth
        attend
To speak with you, may it please you to come down.
  King Richard. Down, down I come, like glist'ring
        Phaëton,
Wanting the manage of unruly jades.
In the base court? Base court, where kings grow
        base,   180
To come at traitors' calls and do them grace!

159 **buried once** once buried. 161 **despised** despicable. 162 **lodge**
beat down. 164 **play the wantons** trifle. 165 **match** competition.
167 **fretted us** worn out for us. 168–9 **there lies . . . eyes** a
mock epitaph. 169 **digg'd** who dug. 171 **laugh** F *mock.* 175 **make a
leg** make a bow. 176 **base court** lower courtyard. 177 **may it**
read 'may't.' 178 **Phaëton** N. 179 **jades** vicious or worthless
horses (here also men?). 181 **grace** honor.

In the base court come down? Down, court! Down,
    king!
For night owls shriek where mounting larks should
    sing.   [*Exeunt from above.*]
    Bullingbrooke. What says his majesty?
    Northumberland.   Sorrow and
    grief of heart
Makes him speak fondly, like a frantic man.   185
Yet he is come.

[*Enter King Richard and his attendants, below.*]

    Bullingbrooke. Stand all apart
And show fair duty to his majesty.   *He kneels down.*
My gracious lord—
    King Richard. Fair cousin, you debase your
    princely knee   190
To make the base earth proud with kissing it.
Me rather had my heart might feel your love
Than my unpleas'd eye see your courtesy.
Up, cousin, up! Your heart is up, I know,
Thus high at least, although your knee be low.   195
    Bullingbrooke. My gracious lord, I come but for
    mine own.
    King Richard. Your own is yours, and I am yours,
    and all.
    Bullingbrooke. So far be mine, my most redoubted
    lord,
As my true service shall deserve your love.

183 **night owls shriek** a death omen. 184 **Sorrow and grief** collective subject. 187 **Stand all apart** everyone stand back. 192
Me . . . had I had rather. 195 **Thus high at least** here Richard
touches his own head. 196 **mine own** what is rightfully mine.
197 is yours because he has taken it. **and all** i.e. and all is yours.
198 **redoubted** dread.

King Richard. Well you deserve. They well deserve
  to have   200
That know the strong'st and surest way to get.
Uncle, give me your hands. Nay, dry your eyes.
Tears show their love but want their remedies.
Cousin, I am too young to be your father,
Though you are old enough to be my heir.   205
What you will have, I'll give, and willing too,
For do we must what force will have us do.
Set on towards London. Cousin, is it so?
  Bullingbrooke. Yea, my good lord.
  King Richard.   Then I must not
  say no.   [*Flourish. Exeunt.*]

SCENE 4

Enter the Queen [and two ladies].

Queen. What sport shall we devise here in this
  garden
To drive away the heavy thought of care?
  Lady. Madam, we'll play at bowls.
  Queen. 'Twill make me think the world is full of
  rubs
And that my fortune runs against the bias.   5
  Lady. Madam, we'll dance.
  Queen. My legs can keep no measure in delight

---

202 **Uncle** addressed to York. **hands** F *Hand*. 203 **want their**
remedies offer no remedies. 204 **Cousin** again addressed to
Bolingbroke. 204–5 **too young . . . heir** N. 208 **is it so?** is that
what you wish? 4 **rubs** obstacles (a bowling term). 5 **bias** the
curve of the ball (a bowling term) N. 7 **measure** formal dance,
or time to music.

When my poor heart no measure keeps in grief.
Therefore no dancing, girl, some other sport.
  Lady. Madam, we'll tell tales.   10
  Queen. Of sorrow or of joy?
  Lady.   Of either, madam.
  Queen. Of neither, girl.
For if of joy, being altogither wanting,
It doth remember me the more of sorrow.
Or if of grief, being altogither had,   15
It adds more sorrow to my want of joy.
For what I have I need not to repeat,
And what I want it boots not to complain.
  Lady. Madam, I'll sing.
  Queen.   'Tis well that thou hast
    cause.
But thou shouldst please me better, wouldst thou
    weep.   20
  Lady. I could weep, madam, would it do you
    good.
  Queen. And I could sing, would weeping do me good,
And never borrow any tear of thee.

    Enter [a gardener and two servants].

But stay, here come the gardeners.
Let's step into the shadow of these trees.   25
My wretchedness unto a row of pins,
They will talk of state, for everyone doth so

8 measure limit. grief other Qq, F; Q *griefs.* 11 joy Qq, F *griefe.*
15 had i.e. present in me. 18 want lack. 26 My wretchedness . . .
pins she will wager her misery against very little (will give liberal
odds). pins Qq *pines;* F *Pinnes.* 27 They will that they will;
read 'they'll'; F *They'le.* state the country's condition.

Against a change. Woe is forerun with woe.

[*Queen and ladies step aside.*]

Gardener. Go bind thou up yon dangling apricocks,
Which, like unruly children, make their sire   30
Stoop with oppression of their prodigal weight.
Give some supportance to the bending twigs.
Go thou and, like an executioner,
Cut off the heads of too fast growing sprays
That look too lofty in our commonwealth.   35
All must be even in our government.
You thus employ'd, I will go root away
The noisome weeds which without profit suck
The soil's fertility from wholesome flowers.   39

Servant. Why should we in the compass of a pale
Keep law and form and due proportion,
Showing, as in a model, our firm estate,
When our sea-walled garden, the whole land,
Is full of weeds, her fairest flowers chok'd up,
Her fruit trees all unprun'd, her hedges ruin'd,   45
Her knots disorder'd, and her wholesome herbs
Swarming with caterpillars?

Gardener.   Hold thy peace.
He that hath suffer'd this disorder'd spring
Hath now himself met with the fall of leaf.
The weeds which his broad-spreading leaves did
    shelter,   50

28 **Against a change** in anticipation of revolution? 29 **yon** other
Qq; Q *yong;* F *yond.* **apricocks** apricots N. 30–66 **Which . . .
thrown down** N. 31 **prodigal** disyllabic. 33 **thou** addressed to the
other servant. 36 **even** neat. 40 **Servant** F; Qq *Man* (also in l. 54).
pale enclosure, walled garden. 41 **proportion** four syllables. 42 **in**
a model in miniature. **firm estate** condition of stability. 46 **knots**
patterned flower beds. **disorder'd** overgrown with weeds. 49 **fall**
of leaf autumn.

That seem'd in eating him to hold him up,
Are pluck'd up root and all by Bullingbrooke—
I mean the Earl of Wiltshire, Bushy, Green.
    Servant. What, are they dead?
    Gardener.   They are, and Bull-
        ingbrooke
Hath seiz'd the wasteful king. O, what pity is it   55
That he had not so trimm'd and dress'd his land
As we this garden! We at time of year
Do wound the bark, the skin of our fruit trees,
Lest, being overproud in sap and blood,
With too much riches it confound itself.   60
Had he done so to great and growing men,
They might have liv'd to bear and he to taste
Their fruits of duty. Superfluous branches
We lop away, that bearing boughs may live.
Had he done so, himself had borne the crown   65
Which waste of idle hours hath quite thrown down.
    Servant. What, think you the king shall be depos'd?
    Gardener. Depress'd he is already, and depos'd
'Tis doubt he will be. Letters came last night
To a dear friend of the good Duke of York's   70
That tell black tidings.
    Queen. O, I am press'd to death through want of
        speaking!
Thou, old Adam's likeness, set to dress this garden,

51 in eating him while actually feeding on him. 52 **pluck'd**
F *pull'd.* 54–7 They are . . . year N. 57 **garden! We at** Qq
garden at; F *Garden, at.* **time** proper time. 58 **Do** F *And.* 59
overproud too luxuriant. **in** other Qq, F *with.* 60 **confound**
destroy. 63 **Superfluous** stressed $\acute{} - \grave{} -$. 66 **of** F *and.* 68
Depress'd humbled. 69 **doubt** perhaps a past participle (see I.4.20–
2 N); F *doubted.* 70 **good** Q, Q2; not in other Qq, F. 72 **press'd**
a legal means of execution; also metaphorical. 73 **Adam's** the
first gardener's.

How dares thy harsh rude tongue sound this un-
    pleasing news?
What Eve, what serpent, hath suggested thee   75
To make a second fall of cursed man?
Why dost thou say King Richard is depos'd?
Dar'st thou, thou little better thing than earth,
Divine his downfall? Say where, when, and how   79
Cam'st thou by this ill tidings? Speak, thou wretch.
   Gardener. Pardon me, madam. Little joy have I
To breathe this news, yet what I say is true.
King Richard, he is in the mighty hold
Of Bullingbrooke. Their fortunes both are weighed.
In your lord's scale is nothing but himself,   85
And some few vanities that make him light;
But in the balance of great Bullingbrooke,
Besides himself, are all the English peers,
And with that odds he weighs King Richard down.
Post you to London and you will find it so.   90
I speak no more than everyone doth know.
   Queen. Nimble Mischance, that art so light of foot,
Doth not thy embassage belong to me,
And am I last that knows it? O, thou think'st
To serve me last, that I may longest keep   95
Thy sorrow in my breast. Come, ladies, go
To meet at London London's king in woe.
What, was I born to this, that my sad look
Should grace the triumph of great Bullingbrooke?

74 How dares . . . news an alexandrine. 75 suggested prompted,
tempted. 76 cursed man see Genesis 3:17–19. 80 Cam'st other
Qq, F; Q *Canst.* 82 this other Qq, F *these.* 90 Post travel posthaste.
you will read 'you'll'; F *you'l.* 93 embassage message. belong
pertain. 96 Thy sorrow the sorrow you report. 99 triumph tri-
umphal procession. great powerful.

Gard'ner, for telling me these news of woe,   100
Pray God the plants thou graft'st may never grow.
                                    Exit [with ladies].
  Gardener. Poor queen, so that thy state might be
    no worse,
I would my skill were subject to thy curse.
Here did she fall a tear; here in this place
I'll set a bank of rue, sour herb of grace.   105
Rue, even for ruth, here shortly shall be seen,
In the remembrance of a weeping queen.   *Exeunt.*

100 **these** F *this.* 101 **Pray God** F *I would.* 102 **so provided that.**
state condition. 104 **fall** let fall; other Qq, F *drop.* 105–6 **rue . . .**
ruth N. 105 **sour** bitter.

85

Act IV

SCENE 1

[*Enter, as to the Parliament, Bullingbrooke, Aumerle, Northumberland, Percy, Fitzwater, Surrey, Bishop of Carlisle, Abbot of Westminster, and another lord, herald, officers, and Bagot.*]

Bullingbrooke. Call forth Bagot.
Now, Bagot, freely speak thy mind:
What thou dost know of noble Gloucester's death,
Who wrought it with the king, and who perform'd
The bloody office of his timeless end.   5

Bagot. Then set before my face the Lord Aumerle.

Bullingbrooke. Cousin, stand forth, and look upon
    that man.

Bagot. My Lord Aumerle, I know your daring
    tongue
Scorns to unsay what once it hath deliver'd.
In that dead time when Gloucester's death was
    plotted,   10
I heard you say, 'Is not my arm of length,
That reacheth from the restful English court
As far as Callice to mine uncle's head?'
Amongst much other talk that very time
I heard you say that you had rather refuse   15

4 **wrought it** worked it, i.e. persuaded the king to order it. 5 **time-less** untimely. 10 **dead** dark and sinister. 11 **of length** long. 12 **restful** peaceful. 13 **Callice** Calais (see I.1.126). 15 **rather refuse** possibly to be read 'rath' refuse.'

86

The offer of an hundred thousand crowns
Than Bullingbrooke's return to England,
Adding withal, how blest this land would be
In this your cousin's death.

   Aumerle.   Princes and noble lords,
What answer shall I make to this base man?   20
Shall I so much dishonor my fair stars
On equal terms to give him chastisement?
Either I must, or have mine honor soil'd
With the attainder of his slanderous lips.
There is my gage, the manual seal of death   25
That marks thee out for hell. I say thou liest,
And will maintain what thou hast said is false
In thy heartblood, though being all too base
To stain the temper of my knightly sword.

   Bullingbrooke. Bagot, forbear. Thou shalt not
    take it up.   30

   Aumerle. Excepting one, I would he were the best
In all this presence that hath mov'd me so.

   Fitzwater. If that thy valor stand on sympathy,
There is my gage, Aumerle, in gage to thine.   34
By that fair sun which shows me where thou stand'st,
I heard thee say, and vauntingly thou spak'st it,
That thou wert cause of noble Gloucester's death.

17–19 Than . . . lords N. 17 Than . . . return than have Bolingbroke return. England trisyllabic. 21 fair stars high birth
and rank, as determined by the stars. 22 to as to. him Q3, F;
Q *them;* Q2 *my.* 24 attainder disgrace, stain. slanderous disyllabic. 25 manual seal sealed warrant (a boast) N. 26 I say
not in other Qq, F. 31 one i.e. Bolingbroke. best noblest. 32
mov'd angered. 33 Fitzwater Walter Fitzwater (or Fitzwalter),
fifth baron. stand on sympathy insist on equality of rank. 34 in
gage to thine mine against yours.

If thou deniest it twenty times, thou liest.
And I will turn thy falsehood to thy heart,
Where it was forged, with my rapier's point.   40

   Aumerle. Thou dar'st not, coward, live to see that
     day.

   Fitzwater. Now, by my soul, I would it were this
     hour.

   Aumerle. Fitzwater, thou art damn'd to hell for
     this.

   Percy. Aumerle, thou liest. His honor is as true
In this appeal as thou art all unjust.   45
And that thou art so, there I throw my gage,
To prove it on thee to the extremest point
Of mortal breathing. Seize it, if thou dar'st.

   Aumerle. And if I do not, may my hands rot off
And never brandish more revengeful steel   50
Over the glittering helmet of my foe!

   Another Lord. I task the earth to the like, forsworn
     Aumerle,
And spur thee on with full as many lies
As may be hollowed in thy treacherous ear
From sun to sun. There is my honor's pawn.   55
Engage it to the trial, if thou dar'st.

   Aumerle. Who sets me else? By heaven, I'll throw
     at all!
I have a thousand spirits in one breast

38 deniest disyllabic. liest monosyllabic. 40 rapier's not used in
England before Shakespeare's day N. 41 live other Qq *live* I.
44 Percy F; Q L[ord] Per[cy]. 45 appeal accusation. 47–8 to
the . . . breathing to your last breath. the extremest read 'th'
extremest.' 51 glittering disyllabic. 52–9 I task . . . as you not
in F. 52 task the earth N. to the like read 't' th' like' (two syllables). 53 lies i.e. charges of lying. 54 As Qq *As it.* hollowed
shouted. 55 sun to sun Qq *sinne to sinne.* 57 sets challenges.
throw at all wager against all that is staked.

To answer twenty thousand such as you.

Surrey. My Lord Fitzwater, I do remember well   60
The very time Aumerle and you did talk.

Fitzwater. 'Tis very true. You were in presence
    then,
And you can witness with me this is true.

Surrey. As false, by heaven, as heaven itself is true!

Fitzwater. Surry, thou liest.

Surrey.   Dishonorable boy!   65
That lie shall lie so heavy on my sword
That it shall render vengeance and revenge
Till thou the lie-giver and that lie do lie
In earth as quiet as thy father's skull.
In proof whereof there is my honor's pawn.   70
Engage it to the trial, if thou dar'st.

Fitzwater. How fondly dost thou spur a forward
    horse!
If I dare eat, or drink, or breathe, or live,
I dare meet Surrey in a wilderness,
And spit upon him whilst I say he lies,   75
And lies, and lies. There is my bond of faith
To tie thee to my strong correction.
As I intend to thrive in this new world,
Aumerle is guilty of my true appeal.
Besides, I heard the banish'd Norfolk say   80
That thou, Aumerle, didst send two of thy men
To execute the noble duke at Callice.

Aumerle. Some honest Christian trust me with a
    gage

---

60 Surrey N. 62 **in presence** in our presence. 65–6 **Dishonorable
. . . sword** F's lineation; one line in Qq. 65 **boy** actually Fitzwater was thirty-one. 76 **my bond** Q3, F; Q *bond;* Q2 *the bond.*
bond of faith gage. 77 **correction** four syllables. 78 **new world**
i.e. under Bolingbroke.

That Norfolk lies. Here do I throw down this,
If he may be repeal'd to try his honor.   85
   Bullingbrooke. These differences shall all rest under
    gage
Till Norfolk be repeal'd. Repeal'd he shall be
And, though mine enemy, restor'd again
To all his lands and signories. When he is return'd,
Against Aumerle we will enforce his trial.   90
   Carlisle. That honorable day shall never be seen.
Many a time hath banish'd Norfolk fought
For Jesu Christ in glorious Christian field,
Streaming the ensign of the Christian cross
Against black pagans, Turks, and Saracens;   95
And toil'd with works of war, retir'd himself
To Italy, and there at Venice gave
His body to that pleasant country's earth
And his pure soul unto his captain Christ,
Under whose colors he had fought so long.   100
   Bullingbrooke. Why, Bishop, is Norfolk dead?
   Carlisle. As surely as I live, my lord.
   Bullingbrooke. Sweet peace conduct his sweet soul
    to the bosom
Of good old Abraham! Lords appellants,
Your differences shall all rest under gage   105
Till we assign you to your days of trial.

Enter York [*, attended*].

---

84 **this** a borrowed hood, according to Holinshed. 85 **repeal'd** re-
called. 86 **differences** trisyllabic (also in l. 105). 89 **signories**
estates (compare III.1.22). **he is** read 'he's'; F *hee's.* 91 **never**
read 'ne'er'; F *ne're.* 96 **toil'd** exhausted. **retir'd himself** withdrew
(compare French *se retirer*). 102 **surely** other Qq, F *sure.* 103–4
bosom . . . Abraham i.e. Paradise (see Luke 16:22). 104 **Lords
appellants** accusing lords.

York. Great Duke of Lancaster, I come to thee
From plume-pluck'd Richard, who with willing soul
Adopts thee heir, and his high scepter yields
To the possession of thy royal hand.   110
Ascend his throne, descending now from him,
And long live Henry, fourth of that name!
  Bullingbrooke. In God's name, I'll ascend the regal
    throne.
  Carlisle. Marry, God forbid!
Worst in this royal presence may I speak,   115
Yet best beseeming me to speak the truth.
Would God that any in this noble presence
Were enough noble to be upright judge
Of noble Richard! Then true noblesse would
Learn him forbearance from so foul a wrong.   120
What subject can give sentence on his king?
And who sits here that is not Richard's subject?
Thieves are not judg'd but they are by to hear,
Although apparent guilt be seen in them.
And shall the figure of God's majesty,   125
His captain, steward, deputy elect,
Anointed, crowned, planted many years,
Be judg'd by subject and inferior breath,
And he himself not present? O, forfend it God
That in a Christian climate souls refin'd   130

108 **plume-pluck'd** broken in power and prestige (compare 'crest-fallen'). 111 **descending . . . him** becoming now his heir. 112 **fourth of that name** F *of that Name the Fourth.* **Henry** read 'Henery.' 114 **Marry** see I.4.16. 115 **Worst** least in rank (or, possibly, least effective). 116 **best** because of his sacred office. 119 **noblesse** other Qq, F *Noblenesse.* 120 **Learn** teach. 123 **but** unless. 124 **apparent** manifest. 127 **planted** established. 129 **forfend** F *forbid.* 130 **refin'd** i.e. by Christianity.

Should show so heinous, black, obscene a deed!
I speak to subjects, and a subject speaks,
Stirr'd up by God, thus boldly for his king.
My Lord of Herford here, whom you call king,
Is a foul traitor to proud Herford's king.   135
And if you crown him, let me prophesy,
The blood of English shall manure the ground
And future ages groan for this foul act.
Peace shall go sleep with Turks and infidels,
And in this seat of peace tumultuous wars   140
Shall kin with kin and kind with kind confound.
Disorder, horror, fear, and mutiny
Shall here inhabit, and this land be call'd
The field of Golgotha and dead men's skulls.
O, if you raise this house against this house,   145
It will the woefullest division prove
That ever fell upon this cursed earth.
Prevent it, resist it, let it not be so,
Lest child, child's children, cry against you 'woe!'
   Northumberland. Well have you argued, sir, and
      for your pains   150
Of capital treason we arrest you here.
My Lord of Westminster, be it your charge
To keep him safely till his day of trial.
May it please you, lords, to grant the commons' suit?
   Bullingbrooke. Fetch hither Richard, that in com-
      mon view   155

131 **obscene** odious (compare Latin *obscenus*). 135 **Herford's king**
i.e. King Richard. 136–47 **And if . . . earth** a prophecy of the
Wars of the Roses. 138 **this** other Qq, F *his*. 144 Golgotha Calvary
(see Matthew 27:33). 145 **raise** rouse; F *reare*. **this house . . .
house** see Matthew 12-25. 148 **Prevent** forestall. **let** other Qq, F
and let. 151 **Of** on a charge of. 154–318 **May it please . . . king's
fall** N. 155–7 **Fetch . . . suspicion** Q4, Q5 give the speech to
Northumberland.

He may surrender. So we shall proceed
Without suspicion.
York.   I will be his conduct.   [*Exit.*]
Bullingbrooke. Lords, you that here are under our
      arrest,
Procure your sureties for your days of answer.
Little are we beholding to your love,   160
And little look'd for at your helping hands.

[*Re-enter York, with Richard, and officers bearing
            the regalia.*]

King Richard. Alack, why am I sent for to a king
Before I have shook off the regal thoughts
Wherewith I reign'd? I hardly yet have learn'd
To insinuate, flatter, bow, and bend my knee.   165
Give Sorrow leave awhile to tutor me
To this submission. Yet I well remember
The favors of these men. Were they not mine?
Did they not sometime cry 'All hail!' to me?
So Judas did to Christ. But He in twelve   170
Found truth in all but one; I in twelve thousand,
      none.
God save the king! Will no man say amen?
Am I both priest and clark? Well then, amen.
God save the king, although I be not he;
And yet amen, if heaven do think him me.   175
To do what service am I sent for hither?

---

156 **surrender** abdicate. 157 **conduct** escort. 158 **here are** Q4, Q5 *are heere, are.* 159 **sureties** bail. 160 **beholding** beholden, indebted. 161 **look'd** Q4, Q5 *looke.* 165 **To insinuate** read 't' insinuate.' **knee** Q4, Q5 *limbes.* 168 **favors** faces, features. 169 **sometime** once; Q4, Q5 *sometimes.* 170 **Judas** see Matthew 26:49. 171 **Found . . . none** an alexandrine. 173 **clark** a parish clerk.

York. To do that office of thine own good will
Which tired majesty did make thee offer:
The resignation of thy state and crown
To Henry Bullingbrooke. 180

    King Richard. Give me the crown. Here, cousin,
        seize the crown.
Here, cousin,
On this side my hand, and on that side thine.
Now is this golden crown like a deep well
That owes two buckets, filling one another, 185
The emptier ever dancing in the air,
The other down, unseen and full of water.
That bucket down and full of tears am I,
Drinking my griefs whilst you mount up on high.

    Bullingbrooke. I thought you had been willing to
        resign. 190

    King Richard. My crown I am, but still my griefs
        are mine.
You may my glories and my state depose,
But not my griefs. Still am I king of those.

    Bullingbrooke. Part of your cares you give me with
        your crown.

    King Richard. Your cares set up do not pluck my
        cares down. 195
My care is loss of care, by old care done.
Your care is gain of care, by new care won.
The cares I give I have, though given away.
They tend the crown, yet still with me they stay.

    Bullingbrooke. Are you contented to resign the
        crown? 200

179 state kingship. 181 **Give me . . . cousin** not in Q4, Q5.
182-3 **Here . . . thine** one line in Q4, Q5, F. 183 and Q4, Q5;
not in F. 185 **owes** owns. 195-9 **Your cares . . . stay** an ex-
tended pun on *care* as trouble and sorrow.

King Richard. I, no—no, I, for I must nothing be.
Therefore no no, for I resign to thee.
Now mark me how I will undo myself.
I give this heavy weight from off my head
And this unwieldy scepter from my hand,   205
The pride of kingly sway from out my heart.
With mine own tears I wash away my balm,
With mine own hands I give away my crown,
With mine own tongue deny my sacred state,
With mine own breath release all duteous oaths.   210
All pomp and majesty I do forswear;
My manors, rents, revenues I forgo;
My acts, decrees, and statutes I deny.
God pardon all oaths that are broke to me!
God keep all vows unbroke are made to thee!   215
Make me, that nothing have, with nothing griev'd,
And thou with all pleas'd, that hast all achiev'd!
Long mayst thou live in Richard's seat to sit,
And soon lie Richard in an earthy pit!
God save King Henry, unking'd Richard says,   220
And send him many years of sunshine days!
What more remains?
    Northumberland.   No more, but that you read
These accusations and these grievous crimes
Committed by your person and your followers
Against the state and profit of this land,   225
That, by confessing them, the souls of men
May deem that you are worthily depos'd.
    King Richard. Must I do so? And must I ravel out

201 I . . . I meaning 'aye' and 'aye' (a pun). 202 no no adjective
and noun. 207 balm holy oil at the coronation. 211 pomp and
majesty hendiadys. 212 revenues stressed — ´ —. 213 deny repeal. 217 thou i.e. thee. 227 worthily justly.

My weav'd-up follies? Gentle Northumberland,
If thy offenses were upon record,   230
Would it not shame thee in so fair a troop
To read a lecture of them? If thou wouldst,
There shouldst thou find one heinous article,
Containing the deposing of a king
And cracking the strong warrant of an oath,   235
Mark'd with a blot, damn'd in the book of heaven.
Nay, all of you that stand and look upon me
Whilst that my wretchedness doth bait myself,
Though some of you with Pilate wash your hands,
Showing an outward pity, yet you Pilates   240
Have here deliver'd me to my sour cross,
And water cannot wash away your sin.
  Northumberland. My lord, dispatch. Read o're
    these articles.
  King Richard. Mine eyes are full of tears. I cannot
    see.
And yet salt water blinds them not so much   245
But they can see a sort of traitors here.
Nay, if I turn mine eyes upon myself,
I find myself a traitor with the rest;
For I have given here my soul's consent
T'undeck the pompous body of a king,   250
Made glory base and sovereignty a slave,
Proud majesty a subject, state a peasant.
  Northumberland. My lord—
  King Richard. No lord of thine, thou haught in-
    sulting man,

230 record stressed — $\stackrel{\prime}{\smile}$. 231 so fair a troop such splendid company (sarcastic). 232 read a lecture of i.e. deliver a moral lesson
from. 235 an oath i.e. Northumberland's oath of allegiance.
238 bait worry, harass N. 239 Pilate see Matthew 27:24–6.
241 sour bitter. 246 sort company, gang. 250 pompous stately,
splendid. 251 and Q4, Q5; F a.

Nor no man's lord. I have no name, no title;   255
No, not that name was given me at the font,
But 'tis usurp'd. Alack the heavy day,
That I have worn so many winters out
And know not now what name to call myself!
O, that I were a mockery king of snow,   260
Standing before the sun of Bullingbrooke
To melt myself away in water drops!
Good king, great king, and yet not greatly good,
And if my word be sterling yet in England,
Let it command a mirror hither straight,   265
That it may show me what a face I have
Since it is bankrupt of his majesty.

Bullingbrooke. Go some of you and fetch a looking
    glass.   [*Exit an attendant.*]

Northumberland. Read o'er this paper while the
    glass doth come.

King Richard. Fiend, thou torments me ere I come
    to hell!   270

Bullingbrooke. Urge it no more, my Lord Northum-
    berland.

Northumberland. The commons will not then be
    satisfied.

King Richard. They shall be satisfied. I'll read
    enough
When I do see the very book indeed
Where all my sins are writ, and that's myself.   275

[*Re-enter an attendant, with a glass.*]

255 Nor Q4, Q5; F *No, nor.* 257 But 'tis usurp'd i.e. he has no
name which is not usurped. 260 **mockery** (disyllabic) mock.
262 To melt . . . drops N. 264 sterling current, valuable. 267 his
its. 268 some some one. SD Exit . . . attendant not in Q4, Q5, F.
270 torments old form of 'tormentest.' SD Re-enter . . . glass
F *Enter one with a Glasse.*

Give me that glass, and therein will I read.
No deeper wrinkles yet? Hath Sorrow struck
So many blows upon this face of mine
And made no deeper wounds? O flatt'ring glass,
Like to my followers in prosperity,   280
Thou dost beguile me! Was this face the face
That every day under his household roof
Did keep ten thousand men? Was this the face
That like the sun did make beholders wink?
Is this the face which fac'd so many follies,   285
That was at last outfac'd by Bullingbrooke?
A brittle glory shineth in this face—
As brittle as the glory is the face,
                              [*Dashes the glass against the ground.*]
For there it is, crack'd in an hundred shivers.
Mark, silent king, the moral of this sport—   290
How soon my sorrow hath destroyed my face.
    Bullingbrooke. The shadow of your sorrow hath
        destroyed
The shadow of your face.
    King Richard.   Say that again.
The shadow of my sorrow! Ha, let's see!
'Tis very true, my grief lies all within,   295
And these external manners of laments
Are merely shadows to the unseen grief
That swells with silence in the tortur'd soul.

276–85 Give me . . . follies N. 280 followers disyllabic. 281–3
Was this . . . men see l. 262 N. 284 wink close their eyes.
285 fac'd countenanced. 287 brittle fragile. SD Dashes . . .
ground not in Q4, Q5, F. 290 sport play acting. 292 shadow
reflection. destroyed i.e. overshadowed. 293 shadow image. 296
external . . . laments outward signs of sorrow. manners Q4,
Q5; F *manner.* 297 shadows to appearances belonging to.

There lies the substance, and I thank thee, king,
For thy great bounty, that not only giv'st   300
Me cause to wail, but teachest me the way
How to lament the cause. I'll beg one boon,
And then be gone and trouble you no more.
Shall I obtain it?
    Bullingbrooke. Name it, fair cousin.
    King Richard. 'Fair cousin'? I am greater than a
      king.   305
For when I was a king, my flatterers
Were then but subjects; being now a subject,
I have a king here to my flatterer.
Being so great, I have no need to beg.
    Bullingbrooke. Yet ask.   310
    King Richard. And shall I have?
    Bullingbrooke. You shall.
    King Richard. Then give me leave to go.
    Bullingbrooke. Whither?
    King Richard. Whither you will, so I were from your
      sights.   315
    Bullingbrooke. Go some of you, convey him to the
      Tower.
    King Richard. O, good! Convey! Conveyers are you
      all
That rise thus nimbly by a true king's fall.
    [*Exeunt King Richard, some lords, and a guard.*]
    Bullingbrooke. On Wednesday next we solemnly set
      down
Our coronation. Lords, prepare yourselves.   320

299 There . . . substance not in Q4, Q5. substance reality,
truth. 308 to for, as. 311 have Q4, Q5 *have it.* 313 Then Q4, Q5
Why then. 315 sights sight (referring to more than one person).
317 Conveyers thieves (a cant term). SD Exeunt . . . guard
not in Q4, Q5, F. 319–20 On . . . yourselves N. 320 coronation N.

Exeunt. Manent [*the Abbot of*] *Westminster,*
[*the Bishop of*] *Carlisle, Aumerle.*

Abbot. A woeful pageant have we here beheld.

Carlisle. The woe's to come. The children yet unborn

Shall feel this day as sharp to them as thorn.

Aumerle. You holy clergymen, is there no plot

To rid the realm of this pernicious blot? 325

Abbot. My lord,

Before I freely speak my mind herein,

You shall not only take the sacrament

To bury mine intents, but also to effect

Whatever I shall happen to devise. 330

I see your brows are full of discontent,

Your hearts of sorrow, and your eyes of tears.

Come home with me to supper. I will lay

A plot shall show us all a merry day. *Exeunt.*

321 **pageant** spectacle. 322 **woe's to come** another prophecy of
the Wars of the Roses (see also III.3.95, IV.1.136). 324 **plot**
plan. 326–7 **My . . . herein** one line in Q, Q2. **My lord** not in F.
332 **hearts** other Qq, F *Heart.* 333–4 **Come . . . plot** one line in
Qq, F. 333 **I will** Qq, F *Ile.* 334 **merry** happy, fortunate.

Act V

SCENE 1

Enter the Queen with her attendants.

Queen. This way the king will come. This is the way
To Julius Caesar's ill-erected tower,
To whose flint bosom my condemned lord
Is doom'd a prisoner by proud Bullingbrooke.
Here let us rest, if this rebellious earth   5
Have any resting for her true king's queen.

Enter King Richard [and guard].

But soft, but see, or rather do not see,
My fair rose wither. Yet look up, behold,
That you in pity may dissolve to dew
And wash him fresh again with true-love tears.   10
Ah, thou the model where old Troy did stand,
Thou map of honor, thou King Richard's tomb,
And not King Richard! Thou most beauteous inn,
Why should hard-favor'd grief be lodg'd in thee
When triumph is become an alehouse guest?   15
  King Richard. Join not with grief, fair woman, do
    not so,

1 Queen N. 2 Caesar's . . . tower legend says Caesar built the
Tower of London. 7 soft be silent a moment. 8 rose i.e. Richard.
9 you i.e. Isabelle herself. 12 map of honor i.e. mere outline of
former glory. 12–13 thou King . . . Richard i.e. his body is the
grave of his kingship. 14 hard-favor'd ill-featured, ugly. 15 alehouse i.e. Bolingbroke (in contrast to Richard, the *beauteous inn*).

To make my end too sudden. Learn, good soul,
To think our former state a happy dream,
From which awak'd, the truth of what we are
Shows us but this. I am sworn brother, sweet,   20
To grim Necessity, and he and I
Will keep a league till death. Hie thee to France
And cloister thee in some religious house.
Our holy lives must win a new world's crown,
Which our profane hours here have thrown down.   25
   Queen. What, is my Richard both in shape and mind
Transform'd and weak'ned? Hath Bullingbrooke de-
     pos'd
Thine intellect? Hath he been in thy heart?
The lion dying thrusteth forth his paw
And wounds the earth, if nothing else, with rage   30
To be orepowr'd. And with thou, pupil-like,
Take thy correction, mildly kiss the rod,
And fawn on rage with base humility,
Which art a lion and the king of beasts?
   King Richard. A king of beasts indeed. If aught but
     beasts,   35
I had been still a happy king of men.
Good sometime queen, prepare thee hence for France.
Think I am dead, and that even here thou tak'st,
As from my deathbed, thy last living leave.
In winter's tedious night sit by the fire   40
With good old folks, and let them tell thee tales
Of woeful ages long ago betid.

20 **this** this wretched state (condition). 25 **our** disyllabic. **profane**
(stressed ― ―) earthly. **thrown** F *stricken.* 27 **Transform'd . . .**
Bullingbrooke one line in Qq, F. 32 **thy** other Qq, F; Q *the.*
34 **Which** who. **the king** other Qq, F *a King.* 37 **sometime** other
Qq, F; Q, Q2 *sometimes.* 38 **even** read 'e'en.' 39 **thy** other Qq, F
my. 42 **betid** happened; other Qq, F *betide.*

And ere thou bid good night, to quite their griefs
Tell thou the lamentable tale of me,
And send the hearers weeping to their beds.   45
For why, the senseless brands will sympathize
The heavy accent of thy moving tongue
And in compassion weep the fire out;
And some will mourn in ashes, some coal-black,
For the deposing of a rightful king.   50

Enter Northumberland [, attended].

Northumberland. My lord, the mind of Bulling-
    brooke is chang'd.
You must to Pomfret, not unto the Tower.
And, madam, there is order tane for you.
With all swift speed you must away to France.
King Richard. Northumberland, thou ladder where-
    withal   55
The mounting Bullingbrooke ascends my throne,
The time shall not be many hours of age
More than it is, ere foul sin gathering head
Shall break into corruption. Thou shalt think,
Though he divide the realm and give thee half,   60
It is too little, helping him to all.
He shall think that thou, which knowest the way
To plant unrightful kings, wilt know again,

43 quite requite, give full return for; F *quit.* griefs other Qq, F
griefe. 44 tale F *fall.* 46 senseless brands i.e. unfeeling logs on the
fire. sympathize respond to; other Qq *sympathy.* 47 moving i.e.
which moves others. 52 Pomfret the common pronunciation (and
occasional spelling) of Pontefract Castle, Yorkshire. 53 order tane
provision made. tane taken. 54 With . . . France N. 55 where-
withal by means of which. 58 gathering head like a boil. gathering
disyllabic. 62 He most editors print *And he* (from Rowe).
knowest F *know'st.*

Being nere so little urg'd, another way
To pluck him headlong from the usurped throne. 65
The love of wicked men converts to fear,
That fear to hate, and hate turns one or both
To worthy danger and deserved death.
    Northumberland. My guilt be on my head, and there
      an end. 69
Take leave and part, for you must part forthwith.
    King Richard. Doubly divorc'd! Bad men, you vio-
      late
A twofold marriage—'twixt my crown and me,
And then betwixt me and my married wife.
Let me unkiss the oath 'twixt thee and me.
And yet not so, for with a kiss 'twas made. 75
Part us, Northumberland, I towards the north
Where shivering cold and sickness pines the clime,
My wife to France, from whence, set forth in pomp,
She came adorned hither like sweet May,
Sent back like Hallowmas or short'st of day. 80
    Queen. And must we be divided? Must we part?
    King Richard. Aye, hand from hand, my love, and
      heart from heart.
    Queen. Banish us both, and send the king with me.
    Northumberland. That were some love, but little
      policy.
    Queen. Then whither he goes, thither let me go. 85
    King Richard. So two, togither weeping, make one
      woe.

65 the usurped read 'th' usurpéd.' 66 men F *friends.* 67–8 turns
. . . death i.e. one wicked man destroys the other, or they
destroy each other. 68 worthy merited. 70 part . . . part separate
. . . depart. 74 oath marriage vow. 77 pines the clime afflicts the
region. 78 wife F *Queene.* pomp splendor. 80 Hallowmas All
Saints' Day (November 1). 84 Northumberland F; Qq give the
line to Richard. policy wisdom.

Weep thou for me in France, I for thee here.
Better far off than near, be nere the near.
Go, count thy way with sighs, I mine with groans.   89
   Queen. So longest way shall have the longest moans.
   King Richard. Twice for one step I'll groan, the
     way being short,
And piece the way out with a heavy heart.
Come, come, in wooing sorrow let's be brief,
Since, wedding it, there is such length to grief.
One kiss shall stop our mouths, and dumbly part.   95
Thus give I mine, and thus take I thy heart.
   Queen. Give me mine own again. 'Twere no good
     part
To take on me to keep and kill thy heart.
So, now I have mine own again, be gone,
That I may strive to kill it with a groan.   100
   King Richard. We make woe wanton with this fond
     delay.
Once more, adieu. The rest let sorrow say.   *Exeunt.*

SCENE 2

Enter the Duke of York and the Duchess.

   Duchess. My lord, you told me you would tell the
     rest,
When weeping made you break the story off
Of our two cousins' coming into London.
   York. Where did I leave?

---

88 **Better** . . . **the near** N. **nere** read 'ne'er' (never). 92 **piece**
the way out lengthen the way. 94 **wedding** becoming attached to.
95 **dumbly part** i.e. shall part us without our saying good-by.
dumbly other Qq *doubly.* 101 **wanton** frivolous. **fond** both loving
and foolish. 3 **two cousins'** i.e. Richard's and Bolingbroke's.

Duchess.   At that sad stop, my lord, 5
Where rude misgovern'd hands from windows' tops
Threw dust and rubbish on King Richard's head.
    York. Then, as I said, the duke, great Bulling-
            brooke,
Mounted upon a hot and fiery steed
Which his aspiring rider seem'd to know,
With slow but stately pace kept on his course,   10
Whilst all tongues cried 'God save thee, Bulling-
            brooke!'
You would have thought the very windows spake,
So many greedy looks of young and old
Through casements darted their desiring eyes
Upon his visage, and that all the walls   15
With painted imagery had said at once
'Jesu preserve thee! Welcome, Bullingbrooke!'
Whilst he, from the one side to the other turning,
Bareheaded, lower than his proud steed's neck,
Bespake them thus, 'I thank you, countrymen.'   20
And thus still doing, thus he pass'd along.
    Duchess. Alack, poor Richard! Where rode he the
            whilst?
    York. As in a theater the eyes of men,
After a well-grac'd actor leaves the stage,
Are idly bent on him that enters next,   25
Thinking his prattle to be tedious,
Even so, or with much more contempt, men's eyes

5 **windows' tops** high windows, probably. 6 **Threw . . . head**
not in the known sources. 9 **Which** subject (not object) of *seem'd*.
16 **painted imagery** human figures on tapestry hangings. 18 **the**
one probably to be read 'th' one'; F *one*. 19 **lower** bending lower.
22 **Alack** F *Alas*. **rode** other Qq, F *rides*. 23 **theater** N. 25 **idly**
indifferently. 27 **Even** read 'e'en.'
    106

Did scowl on gentle Richard. No man cried 'God
    save him!'
No joyful tongue gave him his welcome home,
But dust was thrown upon his sacred head,   30
Which with such gentle sorrow he shook off,
His face still combating with tears and smiles—
The badges of his grief and patience—
That had not God, for some strong purpose, steel'd
The hearts of men, they must perforce have melted
And barbarism itself have pitied him.   36
But heaven hath a hand in these events,
To whose high will we bound our calm contents.
To Bullingbrooke are we sworn subjects now,
Whose state and honor I for aye allow.   40

[*Enter Aumerle.*]

Duchess. Here comes my son Aumerle.
York.   Aumerle that
    was,
But that is lost for being Richard's friend,
And, madam, you must call him Rutland now.
I am in parliament pledge for his truth
And lasting fealty to the new-made king.   45
Duchess. Welcome, my son. Who are the violets now
That strew the green lap of the new-come spring?
Aumerle. Madam, I know not, nor I greatly care
    not.

28 **Did . . . him** an alexandrine. **gentle** not in F. 33 **patience**
trisyllabic. 36 **barbarism itself** even barbarians. 38 **bound** submit.
calm contents proleptic. 40 **for aye allow** accept. 41 **son** stepson,
historically. 43 **Rutland** his new, degraded title as Earl of Rutland.
44 **truth** loyalty. 46 **violets** i.e. court favorites.

God knows I had as lief be none as one.   49

   York. Well, bear you well in this new spring of time,
Lest you be cropp'd before you come to prime.
What news from Oxford? Do these justs and tri-
    umphs hold?

   Aumerle. For aught I know, my lord, they do.

   York. You will be there, I know.

   Aumerle. If God prevent not, I purpose so.   55

   York. What seal is that that hangs without thy
    bosom?
Yea, look'st thou pale? Let me see the writing.

   Aumerle. My lord, 'tis nothing.

   York.   No matter then who
    see it.
I will be satisfied. Let me see the writing.

   Aumerle. I do beseech your grace to pardon me.   60
It is a matter of small consequence
Which for some reasons I would not have seen.

   York. Which for some reasons, sir, I mean to see.
I fear, I fear—

   Duchess.   What should you fear?   64
'Tis nothing but some band that he is ent'red into
For gay apparel 'gainst the triumph day.

   York. Bound to himself! What doth he with a bond
That he is bound to? Wife, thou art a fool.
Boy, let me see the writing.

---

49 had as lief . . . one would be glad not to be one of them.
51 cropp'd both harvested and beheaded. **52–117 What news . . .
gone** for Holinshed's version see Appendix B. **52 Do . . . hold**
F *Hold those Iusts & Triumphs.* **justs and triumphs** tilts (jousts)
and tournaments (see ll. 67–8 N). **hold** take place. **56 seal . . .
hangs** N. **65 band** bond (see l. 67). **66 'gainst the triumph day**
in anticipation of the festal day, here Epiphany (see ll. 67–8 N);
F *against the Triumph* **67–8 Bound . . . bound to** N.

Aumerle. I do beseech you pardon me, I may not
    show it.   70
York. I will be satisfied. Let me see it, I say.
        He plucks it out of his bosom and reads it.
Treason! Foul treason! Villain! Traitor! Slave!
  Duchess. What is the matter, my lord?
  York. Ho! Who is within there? Saddle my horse.
God for His mercy, what treachery is here!   75
  Duchess. Why, what is it, my lord?
  York. Give me my boots, I say. Saddle my horse.
Now, by mine honor, by my life, by my troth,
I will appeach the villain.
  Duchess.   What is the matter?
  York. Peace, foolish woman.   80
  Duchess. I will not peace. What is the matter,
    Aumerle?
  Aumerle. Good mother, be content. It is no more
Than my poor life must answer.
  Duchess.   Thy life answer?
  York. Bring me my boots! I will unto the king.

      His man enters with his boots

  Duchess. Strike him, Aumerle. Poor boy, thou art
    amaz'd.   85
Hence, villain. Never more come in my sight.
  York. Give me my boots, I say!
  Duchess. Why, York, what wilt thou do?
Wilt thou not hide the trespass of thine own?
Have we more sons? Or are we like to have?   90

75 God . . . mercy I pray God for His mercy. 78 by my life . . .
troth other Qq, F *my life, my troth.* 79 **appeach** inform against.
82 **content** calm. 83 **answer** answer for. 85 **him** i.e. the servant.
amaz'd bewildered. 90 **more sons** historically, York had another
son.

Is not my teeming date drunk up with time?
And wilt thou pluck my fair son from mine age
And rob me of a happy mother's name?
Is he not like thee? Is he not thine own?

York. Thou fond mad woman,   95
Wilt thou conceal this dark conspiracy?
A dozen of them here have tane the sacrament,
And interchangeably set down their hands,
To kill the king at Oxford.

Duchess.   He shall be none.
We'll keep him here. Then what is that to him?   100

York. Away, fond woman! Were he twenty times
     my son,
I would appeach him.

Duchess.   Hadst thou groan'd for him
As I have done, thou wouldst be more pitiful.
But now I know my mind. Thou dost suspect
That I have been disloyal to thy bed   105
And that he is a bastard, not thy son.
Sweet York, sweet husband, be not of that mind.
He is as like thee as a man may be,
Not like to me, or any of my kin,   109
And yet I love him.

York.   Make way, unruly woman! *Exit.*

Duchess. After, Aumerle! Mount thee upon his
     horse,

---

91 teeming date drunk up time for childbearing ended. **97 here**
York points to the bond. **98 interchangeably set down** each man
had a copy signed by all. **99–100 He shall . . . here** F's lineation;
one line in Qq. **99 be none** not be one of them. **102–3 Hadst . . .
done** one line in Qq, F. **102 groan'd** i.e. in childbirth. **103 thou
wouldst** read 'thou'dst.' **pitiful** full of pity. **108–9 a . . . any** Q
(Devonshire, Capell, Petworth), other Qq, F; Q (Huth) *any
. . . a.* **111 his horse** one of his horses perhaps N.

Spur post and get before him to the king,
And beg thy pardon ere he do accuse thee.
I'll not be long behind. Though I be old,
I doubt not but to ride as fast as York.   115
And never will I rise up from the ground
Till Bullingbrooke have pardon'd thee. Away, be
    gone!   [*Exeunt.*]

SCENE 3

[*Enter Bullingbrooke, Percy, and other lords.*]

Bullingbrooke. Can no man tell me of my unthrifty
    son?
'Tis full three months since I did see him last.
If any plague hang over us, 'tis he.
I would to God, my lords, he might be found.
Inquire at London, 'mongst the taverns there,   5
For there, they say, he daily doth frequent,
With unrestrained loose companions,
Even such, they say, as stand in narrow lanes
And beat our watch and rob our passengers,
Which he, young wanton and effeminate boy,   10
Takes on the point of honor to support
So dissolute a crew.
    Percy. My lord, some two days since I saw the
    prince

1 Bullingbrooke F; Q *King H[enry]* (throughout the act). me
not in F. son Prince Hal, later Henry V (actually twelve at this
time). 6 frequent intransitive. 7 companions four syllables. 9
beat . . . rob F *rob . . . beat.* watch watchmen. passengers
passers-by. 10 wanton probably a noun. effeminate (trisyllabic)
self-indulgent. 11–12 Takes . . . crew F's lineation; one line in
Qq. 11 Takes on the makes of it a. 12 So . . . crew N.

And told him of those triumphs held at Oxford.
 Bullingbrooke. And what said the gallant?   15
 Percy. His answer was, he would unto the stews,
And from the common'st creature pluck a glove
And wear it as a favor, and with that
He would unhorse the lustiest challenger.
 Bullingbrooke. As dissolute as desperate, yet
  through both   20
I see some sparks of better hope which elder years
May happily bring forth. But who comes here?

    Enter Aumerle, amazed.

 Aumerle. Where is the king?
 Bullingbrooke. What means our cousin, that he
  stares and looks
So wildly?   25
 Aumerle. God save your grace! I do beseech your
  majesty
To have some conference with your grace alone.
 Bullingbrooke. Withdraw yourselves and leave us
  here alone.   [*Exeunt Percy and lords.*]
What is the matter with our cousin now?   29
 Aumerle. Forever may my knees grow to the earth,
My tongue cleave to my roof within my mouth,
Unless a pardon ere I rise or speak.

14 those F *these.* held to be held. 16 stews brothels. 18 favor i.e.
mark of favor. that i.e. the glove. 19 lustiest sturdiest and bravest.
20 both i.e. *dissolute* and *desperate.* 21 I see . . . years an alexandrine. years F *dayes.* 22 happily 'happily' and 'haply.' 23–147
Where is . . . thee new for Holinshed's version see Appendix B.
24–5 What . . . wildly one line in Qq. 27 conference disyllabic.
SD Exeunt . . . lords not in Q, F. 31 My tongue . . . mouth
compare Psalm 137:6.

Bullingbrooke. Intended or committed was this
    fault?
If on the first, how heinous ere it be,
To win thy after-love I pardon thee.   35
  Aumerle. Then give me leave that I may turn the
    key,
That no man enter till my tale be done.
  Bullingbrooke. Have thy desire.
  The Duke of York knocks at the door and crieth.
  York. My liege, beware! Look to thyself!
Thou hast a traitor in thy presence there.   40
  Bullingbrooke. Villain, I'll make thee safe.
                             [*He draws.*]
  Aumerle. Stay thy revengeful hand. Thou hast no
    cause to fear.
  York. Open the door, secure foolhardy king!
Shall I for love speak treason to thy face?
Open the door, or I will break it open!   45

                [*Enter York.*]

  Bullingbrooke. What is the matter, uncle? Speak.
Recover breath, tell us how near is danger,
That we may arm us to encounter it.
  York. Peruse this writing here and thou shalt know
The treason that my haste forbids me show.   50
  Aumerle. Remember, as thou read'st, thy promise
    pass'd.
I do repent me. Read not my name there.
My heart is not confederate with my hand.

36 **I may** other Qq, F; Q *May.* 41 **safe** i.e. harmless. SD **He draws**
not in Q, F. 42 **Stay ... fear** an alexandrine. 43 **secure** heed-
less, overconfident. 44 **speak treason** i.e. abuse the king. 46–7
What ... breath one line in Qq, F. 50 **treason** F *reason.* **haste**
forbids i.e. York is breathless. 53 **confederate** (trisyllabic) a
fellow conspirator with.

York. It was, villain, ere thy hand did set it down.
I tore it from the traitor's bosom, king.   55
Fear, and not love, begets his penitence.
Forget to pity him, lest thy pity prove
A serpent that will sting thee to the heart.

   Bullingbrooke. O heinous, strong, and bold con-
      spiracy!
O loyal father of a treacherous son!   60
Thou sheer, immaculate, and silver fountain,
From whence this stream through muddy passages
Hath held his current and defil'd himself!
Thy overflow of good converts to bad,
And thy abundant goodness shall excuse   65
This deadly blot in thy digressing son.

   York. So shall my virtue be his vice's bawd,
And he shall spend mine honor with his shame,
As thriftless sons their scraping fathers' gold.
Mine honor lives when his dishonor dies,   70
Or my sham'd life in his dishonor lies.
Thou kill'st me in his life. Giving him breath,
The traitor lives, the true man's put to death.

   Duchess. [*Within.*] What ho, my liege! For God's
      sake let me in!

   Bullingbrooke. What shrill-voic'd suppliant makes
      this eager cry?   75

   Duchess. A woman, and thy aunt, great king. 'Tis I.
Speak with me, pity me, open the door!
A beggar begs that never begg'd before.

   Bullingbrooke. Our scene is alt'red from a serious
      thing,

57 to pity to pardon. pity him two syllables. 58 serpent N. 59
strong flagrant. 61 sheer pure and clear. 63 held F *had.* 66 digressing erring. 70 lives i.e. comes to life. 71 in his dishonor lies de-
pends on his dishonor. 75 voic'd other Qq, F; Q, Q2 *voice.* eager
sharp.

And now chang'd to 'The Beggar and the King.'   80
My dangerous cousin, let your mother in.
I know she is come to pray for your foul sin.
　York. If thou do pardon, whosoever pray,
More sins for this forgiveness prosper may.
This fest'red joint cut off, the rest rest sound,   85
This let alone will all the rest confound.

[*Enter Duchess.*]

　Duchess. O king, believe not this hard-hearted man!
Love loving not itself none other can.
　York. Thou frantic woman, what dost thou make
　　here?
Shall thy old dugs once more a traitor rear?   90
　Duchess. Sweet York, be patient. Hear me, gentle
　　liege.
　Bullingbrooke. Rise up, good aunt.
　Duchess. 　　　　　　　　Not yet, I thee
　　beseech.
Forever will I walk upon my knees,
And never see day that the happy sees,
Till thou give joy, until thou bid me joy   95
By pardoning Rutland, my transgressing boy.
　Aumerle. Unto my mother's prayers I bend my
　　knee.
　York. Against them both my true joints bended be.
Ill mayst thou thrive if thou grant any grace!   99

80 **Beggar . . . King** refers to the old ballad 'King Cophetua
and the Beggar Maid.' 82 **she is** read 'she's' as F. 85 **rest rest**
rest remains; F *rest rests.* 88 **Love . . . itself** one (i.e. York) who
loves not his own offspring. 89 **make** do. 93 **walk upon my knees**
a form of penance. **walk** F *kneele.* 96 **Rutland** see V.2.43. 97 **Unto**
in addition to. 99 **Ill . . . grace** not in F.

Duchess. Pleads he in earnest? Look upon his face.
His eyes do drop no tears, his prayers are in jest,
His words come from his mouth, ours from our
    breast.
He prays but faintly and would be denied,
We pray with heart and soul and all beside.
His weary joints would gladly rise, I know,   105
Our knees still kneel till to the ground they grow.
His prayers are full of false hypocrisy,
Ours of true zeal and deep integrity.
Our prayers do outpray his, then let them have
That mercy which true prayer ought to have.   110
   Bullingbrooke. Good aunt, stand up.
   Duchess.   Nay, do not
    say, 'stand up.'
Say 'pardon' first, and afterwards 'stand up.'
And if I were thy nurse, thy tongue to teach,
'Pardon' should be the first word of thy speech.
I never long'd to hear a word till now.   115
Say 'pardon,' king, let pity teach thee how.
The word is short, but not so short as sweet;
No word like 'pardon' for kings' mouths so meet.
   York. Speak it in French, king. Say 'pardonne
    moy.'
   Duchess. Dost thou teach pardon pardon to de-
    stroy?   120
Ah, my sour husband, my hard-hearted lord,
That sets the word itself against the word!

101 **His eyes . . . jest** an alexandrine. 106 **Our . . . grow** compare l. 30 above. **still kneel** shall continue to kneel; F *shall kneele.*
109 **prayers** monosyllabic. 111 **Bullingbrooke** F; Q *yorke.* 112
Say F *But.* 113 **And if** Qq, Ff; most editors print *An if* (old
phrase for 'if'). 119 **pardonne moy** expression of courteous refusal.
pardonne trisyllabic. 121 **sour** bitter.

Speak 'pardon' as 'tis current in our land,
The chopping French we do not understand.
Thine eye begins to speak, set thy tongue there.   125
Or in thy piteous heart plant thou thine ear,
That hearing now our plaints and prayers do pierce,
Pity may move thee 'pardon' to rehearse.
  Bullingbrooke. Good aunt, stand up.
  Duchess.   I do not sue to
    stand.
Pardon is all the suit I have in hand.   130
  Bullingbrooke. I pardon him as God shall pardon
    me.
  Duchess. O happy vantage of a kneeling knee!
Yet am I sick for fear. Speak it again.
Twice saying 'pardon' doth not pardon twain,
But makes one pardon strong.   135
  Bullingbrooke. I pardon him with all my heart.
  Duchess. A god on earth thou art.
  Bullingbrooke. But for our trusty brother-in-law
    and the Abbot,
With all the rest of that consorted crew,
Destruction straight shall dog them at the heels. 140
Good uncle, help to order several powers
To Oxford, or where ere these traitors are.
They shall not live within this world, I swear,

123 **Speak 'pardon'** addressed to the king. 124 **chopping French**
mincing or jerky, such as to change meaning. 125 **speak** i.e.
express pity. 126 **thy** Q (Devonshire, Capell, Petworth), other
Qq, F; Q (Huth) *this*. 128 **rehearse** speak, pronounce. 133 **Yet**
even now (not 'nevertheless'). 136 **I . . . heart** N. 138 **brother-
in-law** the Earl of Huntingdon (formerly Duke of Exeter). **and**
not in F. **Abbot** the Abbot of Westminster. 139 **the rest** about a
dozen (see V.2.97). 141 **order several powers** make ready separate
forces to be sent.

But I will have them, if I once know where.

Uncle, farewell; and cousin, adieu.   145

Your mother well hath pray'd, and prove you true.

  Duchess. Come, my old son. I pray God make thee
    new.   *Exeunt.*

SCENE 4

[Enter Exton and servant.]

  Exton. Didst thou not mark the king, what words
    he spake?

'Have I no friend will rid me of this living fear?'

Was it not so?

  Servant.   These were his very words.

  Exton. 'Have I no friend?' quoth he. He spake it
    twice

And urg'd it twice togither, did he not?   5

  Servant. He did.

  Exton. And speaking it, he wishtly look'd on me,

As who should say, 'I would thou wert the man

That would divorce this terror from my heart,'

Meaning the king at Pomfret. Come, let's go.   10

I am the king's friend, and will rid his foe. *[Exeunt.]*

---

145 cousin Qq, F; most editors print *cousin too* from Q6 (1634).
145–7 adieu . . . true . . . new triple rhyme (rare in Shakespeare, but see V.5.95–7). SD Enter . . . servant N. 1–11 Didst
. . . foe for Holinshed's version see Appendix B. 3 Servant F;
Q *Man* (also in l. 6). These F *Those.* 7 wishtly probably means
'longingly' (compare 'wishly' and 'whistly' in OED); Q3, Q4, Q5,
F *wistly*, closely, attentively. 8 As who as one who.

SCENE 5

Enter [King] Richard, alone.

King Richard. I have been studying how I may
    compare
This prison where I live unto the world.
And for because the world is populous
And here is not a creature but myself,
I cannot do it. Yet I'll hammer it out.   5
My brain I'll prove the female of my soul,
My soul the father, and these two beget
A generation of still-breeding thoughts,
And these same thoughts people this little world
In humors like the people of this world,   10
For no thought is contented. The better sort,
As thoughts of things divine, are intermix'd
With scruples, and do set the word itself
Against the word,
As thus: 'Come, little ones,' and then again,   15
'It is as hard to come as for a camel
To thread the postern of a small needle's eye.'
Thoughts tending to ambition, they do plot

1 **I may** other Qq, F *to*. 3 **for because** because (a reduplication).
5 **hammer it** read 'hammer't' as F; worry it. 8 **still** constantly.
9 **this little world** both his microcosm (self) and his prison. 10
humors see I.1.153 N. 13 **scruples** doubts, difficulties. 13–14
word . . . word i.e. contradictions in Scripture; F *Faith . . .
Faith.* 14–15 **Against . . . again** one line in Qq, F. 15 **Come,
little ones** see Matthew 19:14. 16–17 **It is . . . eye** see Matthew
19:24. 17 **thread** Q5; other Qq *threed*; F *thred.* **postern** small back
gate, i.e. opening. **small** not in F. *needle's* monosyllabic (read
'neeld' or 'neel'). 18 **they** redundant.

Unlikely wonders—how these vain weak nails
May tear a passage through the flinty ribs   20
Of this hard world, my ragged prison walls,
And, for they cannot, die in their own pride.
Thoughts tending to content flatter themselves
That they are not the first of fortune's slaves,
Nor shall not be the last, like seely beggars   25
Who sitting in the stocks refuge their shame,
That many have and others must sit there.
And in this thought they find a kind of ease,
Bearing their own misfortunes on the back
Of such as have before endur'd the like.   30
Thus play I in one person many people,
And none contented. Sometimes am I king,
Then treasons make me wish myself a beggar,
And so I am. Then crushing penury
Persuades me I was better when a king.   35
Then am I king'd again. And by and by
Think that I am unking'd by Bullingbrooke,
And straight am nothing. But what ere I be,
Nor I nor any man that but man is
With nothing shall be pleas'd till he be eas'd   40
With being nothing. Music do I hear?

The music plays.

20–1 **May tear . . . walls** compare III.3.32. 21 **ragged** rugged.
22 **for they cannot** since the nails cannot die. **in . . . pride** i.e.
in their prime. 25 **seely** old form of 'silly,' or pitiful; F *silly*.
26 **refuge** stressed — ´. **refuge their shame** find refuge from
their shame in the thought. 29 **misfortunes** F *misfortune*. 31
person other Qq, F *Prison*. 33 **treasons make** F *Treason makes*.
34 **so I am** so I become one (in my imagination). 36 **king'd** Q2
king; other Qq *a king*. 38 **be** F *am*. 39 **man is** is a man. 41 **being
nothing** i.e. dying. SD **The music** F *Music* (F's direction at l. 38).

120

Ha, ha! Keep time. How sour sweet music is
When time is broke and no proportion kept!
So is it in the music of men's lives.
And here have I the daintiness of ear   **45**
To check time broke in a disorder'd string,
But for the concord of my state and time
Had not an ear to hear my true time broke.
I wasted time, and now doth time waste me;
For now hath time made me his numb'ring clock.   **50**
My thoughts are minutes, and with sighs they jar
Their watches on unto mine eyes, the outward watch,
Whereto my finger, like a dial's point,
Is pointing still, in cleansing them from tears.
Now, sir, the sound that tells what hour it is   **55**
Are clamorous groans which strike upon my heart,
Which is the bell. So sighs and tears and groans
Show minutes, times, and hours. But my time
Runs posting on in Bullingbrooke's proud joy,
While I stand fooling here, his Jack of the clock.   **60**
This music mads me. Let it sound no more,
For though it have holp mad men to their wits,
In me it seems it will make wise men mad.
Yet blessing on his heart that gives it me!
For 'tis a sign of love, and love to Richard   **65**

43 **proportion** rhythm. 46 **check** find fault with; F *heare*. 47 **time**
life. 50–8 **For now . . . hours** N. 50 **numb'ring clock** clock that
marks hours and minutes (not an hourglass). 51 **jar** tick. 52
Their . . . watch an alexandrine. **watches** marks for minutes on
a dial. 53 **dial's point** clock hand. 56 **which** F *that*. 58 **times**
divisions of quarter- and half-hours. **times, and hours** F *Houres,*
and Times. **hours** disyllabic. 60 **Jack of the clock** N. 61–2 **This**
music . . . wits an ancient cure (see Samuel 16:16, also *King*
Lear, IV.7.25). 62 **holp** helped. **mad men** F *madmen*.

Is a strange brooch in this all-hating world.

Enter a groom of the stable.

Groom. Hail, royal prince!

King Richard.   Thanks, noble peer.

The cheapest of us is ten groats too dear.

What art thou? And how comest thou hither

Where no man never comes but that sad dog   70

That brings me food to make misfortune live?

Groom. I was a poor groom of thy stable, king,

When thou wert king, who, traveling towards York,

With much ado at length have gotten leave

To look upon my sometimes royal master's face.   75

O, how it ern'd my heart when I beheld

In London streets, that coronation day,

When Bullingbrooke rode on roan Barbary,

That horse that thou so often hast bestrid,

That horse that I so carefully have dress'd!   80

King Richard. Rode he on Barbary? Tell me, gentle friend,

How went he under him?

Groom. So proudly as if he disdain'd the ground.

King Richard. So proud that Bullingbrooke was on his back!

That jade hath eat bread from my royal hand,   85

This hand hath made him proud with clapping him.

---

66 **brooch** ornament. **all-hating** i.e. which utterly hates Richard (or which hates all men). 67 **royal, noble** puns N. 70 **never** F *euer.* 73 **traveling towards** four syllables (read 'traveling tord' or 'trav'l-ing towards'). 76 **ern'd** grieved; F *yern'd*, moved to compassion. 78 **Barbary** part of northwest Africa famous for horses. 79 **bestrid** bestrode, mounted; F; Qq *bestride.* 80 **dress'd** groomed. 83 **he** F *he had.* 85 **jade** see III.3.179. **eat** eaten. 86 **clapping** patting.

Would he not stumble? Would he not fall down—
Since pride must have a fall—and break the neck
Of that proud man that did usurp his back?
Forgiveness, horse! Why do I rail on thee, 90
Since thou, created to be aw'd by man,
Wast born to bear? I was not made a horse,
And yet I bear a burthen like an ass,
Spurr'd, gall'd, and tir'd by jauncing Bullingbrooke.

[Enter keeper, with a dish.]

Keeper. Fellow, give place. Here is no longer stay.
King Richard. If thou love me, 'tis time thou wert
away. 96
Groom. What my tongue dares not, that my heart
shall say. *Exit groom.*
Keeper. My lord, will't please you to fall to?
King Richard. Taste of it first, as thou art wont to
do.
Keeper. My lord, I dare not. Sir Pierce of
Exton, 100
Who lately came from the king, commands the con-
trary.
King Richard. The divel take Henry of Lancaster,
and thee!
Patience is stale, and I am weary of it.
[Beats the keeper.]
Keeper. Help, help, help!
[Exton and servants,] the murderers, rush in.

88 pride . . . fall see Proverbs 16:18. 94 Spurr'd, gall'd F *Spur-
gall'd.* jauncing making the horse prance (participial adjective).
95–118 Fellow . . . here for Holinshed's version see Appendix B.
95–7 stay . . . away . . . say triple rhyme. 99 art F *wer't.* 101
Who . . . contrary probably an alexandrine. the king F *th' King.*
102 divel devil. SD Beats . . . keeper not in Q, F.

King Richard. How now! What means Death in
   this rude assault?   105
Villain, thy own hand yields thy death's instrument.
Go thou and fill another room in hell.
                              Here Exton strikes him down.
That hand shall burn in never-quenching fire,
That staggers thus my person. Exton, thy fierce
   hand
Hath with the king's blood stain'd the king's own
   land.   110
Mount, mount, my soul! Thy seat is up on high,
Whilst my gross flesh sinks downward, here to die.
                                                          [Dies.]

Exton. As full of valor as of royal blood.
Both have I spill'd. O, would the deed were good!
For now the divel, that told me I did well,   115
Says that this deed is chronicl'd in hell.
This dead king to the living king I'll bear.
Take hence the rest, and give them burial here.
                                                          [Exeunt.]

SCENE 6

*[Flourish.] Enter Bullingbrooke with the Duke
     of York [, lords, and attendants].*

Bullingbrooke. Kind uncle York, the latest news we
     hear
Is that the rebels have consum'd with fire
Our town of Ciceter in Gloucestershire,

107 room place, space. 112 die N. SD Dies not in Q, F. 114 spill'd
Holinshed says Exton wept bitterly. 118 burial disyllabic. 1
latest news N. 3 Ciceter this (or Cicester) is the local pronunciation of Cirencester.

124

But whether they be tane or slain we hear not.

Enter Northumberland.

Welcome, my lord. What is the news? 5
Northumberland. First, to thy sacred state wish I
all happiness.
The next news is, I have to London sent
The heads of Oxford, Salisbury, Blunt, and Kent.
The manner of their taking may appear
At large discoursed in this paper here. 10
Bullingbrooke. We thank thee, gentle Percy, for
thy pains,
And to thy worth will add right worthy gains.

Enter Lord Fitzwater.

Fitzwater. My lord, I have from Oxford sent to
London
The heads of Broccas and Sir Bennet Seely,
Two of the dangerous consorted traitors 15
That sought at Oxford thy dire overthrow.
Bullingbrooke. Thy pains, Fitzwater, shall not be
forgot.
Right noble is thy merit, well I wot.

Enter Henry Percy [and Carlisle].

Percy. The grand conspirator, Abbot of West-
minster,
With clog of conscience and sour melancholy 20
Hath yielded up his body to the grave.
But here is Carlisle living, to abide

4 **tane or slain** internal rhyme. 6 **state** royalty. 8 **Oxford** . . .
Kent N. 14 **Broccas** Holinshed: 'Sir Leonard [should be 'Bernard']
Brokas.' **Seely** Holinshed: 'Sir Benet Cilie.' 20 **clog** burden,
weight. 22 **abide** await.

Thy kingly doom and sentence of his pride.

Bullingbrooke. Carlisle, this is your doom: 24
Choose out some secret place, some reverent room,
More than thou hast, and with it joy thy life.
So as thou liv'st in peace, die free from strife.
For though mine enemy thou hast ever been,
High sparks of honor in thee have I seen.

Enter Exton, with [attendants bearing] the coffin.

Exton. Great king, within this coffin I present   30
Thy buried fear. Herein all breathless lies
The mightiest of thy greatest enemies,
Richard of Bordeaux, by me hither brought.

Bullingbrooke. Exton, I thank thee not, for thou
    hast wrought
A deed of slander, with thy fatal hand,   35
Upon my head and all this famous land.

Exton. From your own mouth, my lord, did I this
    deed.

Bullingbrooke. They love not poison that do poison
    need,
Nor do I thee. Though I did wish him dead,
I hate the murtherer, love him murthered.   40
The guilt of conscience take thou for thy labor,
But neither my good word nor princely favor.

---

23 **doom** judgment. **of** on. 25 **reverent room** sacred place; F
reuerend, worthy of respect. **reverent** disyllabic. 29 **High** noble.
SD **attendants bearing** not in Q, F. 33 **Bordeaux** stressed $\smile$ —;
Qq, F *Burdeaux*. 34–44 **Exton . . . light** this repudiation not in
the known sources. 35 **deed of slander** deed bringing censure and
disgrace. **slander** other Qq, F *slaughter*. 40 **murtherer** read
'murth'rer.' **him murthered** him who is murdered.

With Cain go wander through shades of night,
And never show thy head by day nor light.
Lords, I protest my soul is full of woe   45
That blood should sprinkle me to make me grow.
Come, mourn with me for what I do lament,
And put on sullen black incontinent.
I'll make a voyage to the Holy Land
To wash this blood off my guilty hand.   50
March sadly after, grace my mournings here
In weeping after this untimely bier.   [*Exeunt.*]

43 **Cain** see Genesis 4:12, 14. **through** read 'thorough.' **shades**
other Qq, F *the shade*. 48 **sullen** mournful. **incontinent** at once. 49
voyage . . . Land links with 1 *Henry IV*, I.1.18–27. 51 **sadly**
solemnly. **grace** do honor to. **mournings** F *mourning*. 52 **bier** N.

NOTES

The Actors' . . . **Wales** Neither a list of characters nor notation of scene appears in the Qq or Ff. (Qq refers throughout to the
five quartos printed between 1597 and 1615, and Ff to the four
folios printed between 1623 and 1685.) The list of characters
and notation of scene were first printed by Nicholas Rowe (1709),
who is followed here, though with small additions from Edward
Capell (1768) and minor alterations in line with W. A. Wright's
Cambridge edition (1891).

Act I, Scene 1

Act I, Scene 1 Since no act or scene divisions appear in the Qq,
they are (with the one exception noted at V.4.1SD) taken from F.

1SD King Richard Richard of Bordeaux (1367–1400), son of
Edward the Black Prince. Although the play reaches back into
earlier events, the action proper (which begins when Richard is
just over thirty) covers only the last two years of his life. A
decade earlier Richard had chosen five newly created peers as
his favorites, which caused five established members of the
nobility (Gloucester, Arundel, Warwick, Mowbray, and Bolingbroke) to accuse the favorites of treason. Overruling Richard,
the parliament forthwith judged against his men, of whom two
fled and three were put to death. But by 1397 Richard took firmer
control and proceeded to arrest Gloucester, Arundel, and Warwick on old charges. All three were soon dead or banished. The
remaining two lords, Mowbray and Bolingbroke, by now enjoying
the titles of Duke of Norfolk and Duke of Hereford, were re-
gaining some of their old eminence. But a quarrel then arose
between them over the way Richard was treating his great nobles.
According to Holinshed (whose generally accurate historical picture is closely followed by Shakespeare), Bolingbroke rose before
the assembled parliament at Shrewsbury and accused Mowbray
of treason. He charged that Mowbray, while riding with him from
London to Brainford, spoke 'highlie to the kings dishonor.'
Though Mowbray was not present when the charge was first made,

he was later on hand to answer it before parliament. The action of the play begins in April 1398, several weeks after the episode at Shrewsbury. The two lords are being heard by Richard and the parliament at Windsor. Historically, Bolingbroke's accusation seems not to have involved questions of peculation, treasonous plots, and participation in Gloucester's murder, as it does here. But dramatically Shakespeare has designed to show Bolingbroke's action as his first move toward the crown in this drama of deposition, though just how deliberate that first move is, even within the play itself, is a matter of controversy.

1 **John of Gaunt** John of Gaunt (corrupted from the French *Gand*, i.e. Ghent, were he was born) is fifty-eight and his brother York is fifty-seven. Above and beyond the Elizabethan inclination to view anyone over fifty as 'old,' Shakespeare makes a particularly sharp contrast between the age of these two figures and the 'youth' of the king (II.1.69).

3 **Herford** Hereford (usually spelled *Herford* in Qq and F) was Henry Plantagenet (1367–1413), called Bolingbroke from the castle in Leicestershire where he was born, although he did not actually adopt this surname until his accession.

12 **As near . . . argument** Although twelve-syllable lines may be read as alexandrines (six-stress lines), they are often more easily read with five stresses, not uncommonly with the final two syllables sounded very lightly. As a rule, alexandrine lines are few in the early plays—*Romeo and Juliet* has none at all—and quite numerous in the later. But this play, which has over thirty, is an exception.

20 **Bullingbrooke** This, the usual spelling of Bolingbroke in Qq and F, indicates also the pronunciation of the name.

20 **Many . . . befall** The line is metrically short, but omission of a weak opening syllable is a normal verse variation, perhaps sometimes allowing for an actor's expressive pause, and need not be filled in. (It should be remembered that while metrical regularity is usual in the play, variations are to be expected here as well as in other plays presumed to have been set directly from Shakespeare's own manuscript.)

34 **appellant** 'Accuser' (noun) or 'bringing accusation' (ad-

jective). If read as a noun, the word is almost a technical term for 'challenger' (see I.3.4, 52; IV.1.104).

63 tied In order to indicate pronunciation in this edition, unaccented syllables concluding certain past tenses, past participles, and verbs inflected in the second-person singular of the present tense are printed with an apostrophe (e.g. *receiv'd*, *time-honor'd*, *high-stomach'd*, *com'st*, *think'st*), regardless of their forms in the copy texts. Certain other verbs, however, and especially those ending in *-ied*, are printed in full because their final syllables are usually not accented (e.g. *tied*, *denied*, *lied;* also *baffled*, *rued*, *settled*).

77 thou . . . devise So reads Q; Q2, F read *thou canst devise;* other Qq read *what thou canst devise*. Obviously after *worse* was dropped out in Q2, later versions attempted to make up the loss. Though the original meaning is not entirely clear, two interpretations at least are possible. *Or thou canst worse devise* may conclude the idea 'those treasonous acts that I say you have done, *or that you are capable of doing.*' On the other hand, if one agrees with H. H. Vaughan and Sir Edmund Chambers to take *or* to mean 'before,' the sense is 'before you can devise worse treasons.'

100 Duke of Gloucester's death Thomas Woodstock, Duke of Gloucester and youngest son of Edward III, was murdered when in the custody of Mowbray (then Earl of Nottingham) at Calais in 1397. Though proof is lacking, it was then assumed, and still is, that Richard gave orders for Mowbray to carry out the murder.

101–3 Suggest . . . blood J. Dover Wilson asserts (though Peter Ure in the New Arden edition disagrees) that since Holinshed, Froissart, and the other French authorities say that Gloucester was strangled by towels and/or smothered in a feather-bed, Shakespeare has followed 'Jean Le Beau' in *La Chronique de Richard II*, who says that Gloucester was beheaded. (See I.2.21, II.2.102, and Appendix B.)

119 neighbor nearness Though the F reading, *neighbour-neerenesse*, makes *neighbor* a noun, it may be an adjective. In Shakespeare's time the parts of speech were not treated so strictly as they were even later in the 17th century. Very frequently he uses adjectives as nouns, nouns as verbs, and so forth.

Compare *exclaims* (I.2.2), *venom* (II.1.19), *ague* (III.2.190), *sooth* (III.3.136), *sunshine* (IV.1.221), *mockery* (IV.1.260), *true-love* (V.1.10), *triumph* (V.2.66), *peace* (V.2.81).

119 **sacred blood** Here for the first time Richard strikes a note that rings throughout his speeches: divine right of kings, which in Richard's mind (as A. W. Verity observes in his edition, 1899) always refers not to the responsibilities but to the privileges of kingship.

131 **queen** In 1395 a mission went to France to negotiate the marriage between Richard and Isabelle, the daughter of King Charles VI of France. Although she was only eight at the time, in the play she is treated as an adult.

135–41 **For you . . . it** Here is one of the occasions on which Shakespeare has (except in l. 139) followed Holinshed very closely. Holinshed: 'True it is that once I laid an ambush to have slain the Duke of Lancaster that there sitteth; but nevertheless he hath pardoned me thereof, and there was good peace made betwixt us, for the which I yield him hearty thanks.' No other record of this incident has yet been discovered.

153 **choler** Here the word seems also to have taken on its meaning as one of the four 'humors.' In ancient and medieval physiology and (what we now call) psychology, a man's health and temperament were thought to be determined by the relative amounts of the four fluids in his body: blood, melancholy (or black bile), choler (or yellow bile), and phlegm. These four, corresponding to the four elements in nature—air, earth, fire, and water—were thought to operate in such a way that an excess of air (blood) produced a sanguine man, of earth a melancholic man, of fire a choleric man, and of water a phlegmatic man.

157 **no month to bleed** Elizabethan almanacs, e.g. *The Prognostycacion for ever of Erra Pater* (1602), explain, often in elaborate detail, what seasons are proper for the success of bleeding, pulling teeth, cutting hair, and more. April was the favorite month for bleeding, though evidently not in this case (which may be why the Ff read *time* and not *month* as in Qq).

174 **lions . . . leopards** Basically the lion may be thought of as the emblem of English kings, and the golden leopard as the Mowbray crest. A more refined explanation is offered, however,

in C. W. Scott-Giles, *Shakespeare's Heraldry* (London, Dutton, 1950), p. 75: 'In heraldic language, the lion rampant of Mowbray could not be called a leopard, but this term might be applied to the lion statant forming his crest, the lion in any attitude but rampant having been termed a leopard, or *lion leopardé*, in ancient heraldry. If, to point the king's words, it is decided to give Norfolk a crested helm for this scene, the beast forming the crest should be the stylized heraldic lion, not spotted or otherwise made to resemble the natural leopard.'

176 gage. My dear Some variation in meaning is occasioned within this line by variations in punctuation. The punctuation printed here is from F; Q, Q4, and Q5 read *gage, my deare*, and Q2, Q3 read *gage my deare*.

186 throw up Wilson thinks this means throw it up 'to the scaffold (upper stage) on which Ric[hard] and his nobles sit.' But most scholars (including C. J. Sisson, *New Readings in Shakespeare*, Cambridge, Cambridge University Press, 1956, *2*, 15) prefer F's *throw downe*. (For descriptions of the different stages of various Elizabethan public theaters, see C. Walter Hodges, *The Globe Restored*, London, Ernest Benn, 1953.)

187 God To comply with 'An Act to restrain the abuses of the Players' passed by James I in 1606, F nearly always substitutes *heauen* for Q's *God*.

192 sound . . . parle A metaphor for sounding a trumpet (or beating a drum) to talk over terms—in this case, the terms of a shameful truce. (The form *parle* is taken from F; Qq read *parlee*.)

195SD Exit Gaunt This awkward exit (in F but not in Qq) is essential to Gaunt's entrance again at the opening of the next scene. (*Note:* Although stage directions for the present edition come mainly from Q, countless minor alterations are made without being noted. However, since the directions in F are more numerous, more complete, and more accurate than those in Q, many of them have been adopted and are printed in square brackets. The exception to the adequacy of F's directions is the 'deposition scene' (IV.1.154–318), in which their absence or incompleteness has been compensated for from Capell and Lewis Theobald.)

204 **Marshal** Thomas Holland, Duke of Surrey. The second syllable may be read lightly, or *Marshal* may be read as three syllables and the line as an alexandrine.

Act I, Scene 2

1 **blood** Here *blood* possibly means 'murder' since, as the argument runs in the edition of Henry Irving and Frank A. Marshall (1888–90), 'Lancaster was certainly privy to the proceedings against his brother,' as he was to those against his son.

11 **Edward's seven sons** Besides the Duchess' dead husband, Thomas of Woodstock, Duke of Gloucester (1355–97), they are: King Richard's father, Edward the Black Prince (1330–76); William of Hatfield (1336–44); Lionel of Antwerp, Duke of Clarence (1338–68); John of Gaunt (1340–99); Edmund of Langley, Duke of York (1341–1402); and William of Windsor, who died in infancy.

14–21 **Some . . . ax** Of the five dead sons, the Duchess is saying, four died of natural causes while the fifth, Gloucester, was murdered.

30 **slaught'red** There is some question about the pronunciation of several verbs which in Q show elision of the next to last syllable, as here, rather than the last. In this edition the Q forms have been preserved; the other instances in addition to *slaught'red* are: *wand'red* (I.3.195), *length'ned* (I.4.16), *off'red* (II.1.204), *sweet'ned* (II.3.13), *weak'ned* (V.1.27), *ent'red* (V.2.65), *alt'red* (V.3.79), and *fest'red* (V.3.85). For such forms see Helge Kökeritz, *Shakespeare's Pronunciation* (New Haven, Yale University Press, 1953), pp. 262–3, who argues convincingly that two alternative pronunciations existed in Shakespeare's time.

42 **then, alas, may** Significant variations within the four extant copies of Q, labeled Huth, Capell, Devonshire, and Petworth, are cited in the glosses. (See Appendix A.) In all instances readings from the 'corrected' sheets precede those from the 'uncorrected.'

44 **Why then . . . Gaunt** Possibly this is a pentameter line whose shortness could be accounted for by prolonging *will* and reading *Farewell* as trisyllabic (it comes from 'fare ye well').

But probably the line is a tetrameter, of which Shakespeare wrote a good number when shifting to a new idea, especially at a speech's beginning or end.

46 cousin In Shakespeare the word indicates almost any sort of kindship except the closest (like father or brother).

58-9 Grief . . . weight Like a ball, her grief falls (subsides) only to rebound (surge up again), though not lightly like a ball.

Act I, Scene 3

6SD enter Mowbray, Strictly speaking, the appellant Bolingbroke (who is challenging) should appear in the lists first. (For deviations from the stage directions in Q, see I.1.195SD N.)

11 say who thou art This formality was not altogether empty. Since a knight's crest might not be known and his beaver (visor) was down over his face, identification was sometimes necessary. Furthermore the question calls forth a statement of rank, and no knight was obliged to fight with anyone inferior in rank.

15 As so defend Some editors merely change *as* to *and*, although all Qq and Ff read *as*. It may be that before using the ordinary formula for oaths, which began with 'so' (see I.3.34), the Marshal first started out in a less usual way with *as*, or else that he used *as* in another sense, in effect ordering Richard to 'speak truly . . . in this fashion: so defend thee.'

20 my succeeding Sisson, *New Readings in Shakespeare, 2,* 16–17, regards F's *his succeeding* as a true correction since the usual oath is to God, the king, and the king's heirs and successors.

84 Mine . . . George This prayer to Saint George, patron saint of England, implies that a true patriot (Bolingbroke) is protecting his king and country against a traitor (Mowbray). Before *Mine* one must supply something like 'I pray.'

193 so far . . . enemy 'This much do I say to you my enemy.' But the line is obscure since Qq and F read *fare*, with *far* appearing only in the other Ff. Some editors follow George Tollet's explanation (Variorum edition, 1778): 'He only wishes him to *fare* like his enemy, and he disdains to say *fare* well.'

211 Pluck'd four away Holinshed says the sentence was reduced, but some weeks later, in Eltham. Anthony Steel, however, in *Richard II* (Cambridge, Cambridge University Press, 1941), p. 253, says that Richard, although not daring to ignore Bolingbroke's popularity on the occasion when he passed sentence, six months later increased the ten-year banishment to a sentence of life.

248SD **Flourish . . . train** 'We have here an illustration how the absence of scenery on the Elizabethan stage affected the structure of plays. In a modern play, surely, this scene would end with the king's exit. The interview between Gaunt and Bolingbroke would be thrown into a fresh scene. For characters to remain behind and wind up a scene seems unnatural; it risks an anticlimax. But in the Elizabethan theatre, as there was no curtain to fall and practically no scenery to mark a change of scene, the tendency was to extend a scene instead of starting a fresh one: as if the playwright thought that certain characters might as well stay behind as go off and return' (A. W. Verity, Cambridge edition, 1899).

249–50 **What . . . show** 'What you cannot tell us in person, tell us by letter, wherever you may be' (although *presence* may mean, as Hardin Craig says in *Complete Works*, Chicago, Scott, Foresman, 1951, 'presence chamber at Court').

266 **foil** Refers to the gold leaf set behind a jewel to increase its brilliance.

289 **strow'd** It was an Elizabethan custom to strew the royal presence chamber with rushes (sometimes mixed with herbs).

Act I, Scene 4

1SD **Green and Bagot** So F, while Q reads *with Bushie &c,* which is impossible since Bushy does not enter until l. 52.

20–2 **doubt . . . friends** *Doubt* may be a noun (meaning 'a matter of doubt') or a past participle (meaning 'suspected' or 'feared'). The sense of the lines seems to be that Richard expects Bolingbroke to return as an enemy, but more probably that Richard will see to it that he does not return.

23 **Ourself . . . Green** So reads F (though differently punctuated), but many editors reject both F and the shorter reading of the other Qq, *Our selfe and Bushie*, in favor of Q6 (1634):

Our selfe and Bushie, Bagot here and Greene. Incidentally, the popular poetry of the period refers to the three as 'the Bush,' 'the Bag,' and 'the Green,' who do in 'the Swan' (Gloucester) and are then punished by 'the Eagle' (Bolingbroke). (For historical identifications see II.1.68SD N.)

43–4 court . . . largess According to the chroniclers Richard's extravagance was notorious. It was said that he spent for his own purposes one third of the total national expenditure of £137,900. He himself boasts of keeping 10,000 retainers (IV.1.283); Holinshed writes that he wore 'a coat of gold and stone valued at 30,000 marks' (a possible error for 3,000); and a poem of the time (by Langland?), *On the Deposition of King Richard*, observes:

> For where was ever any Christian king
> That held such an household by the half-deal
> As Richard in his realm, through misrule of others.

Nevertheless, recent historians believe the records to show no such excess and abuse, and one of them draws quite another portrait of Richard as a tortured, melancholic, and highly neurotic figure (Anthony Steel, *Richard II*, pp. 173–5, 216, 278–9).

45 farm . . . realm As the lines following all but explain, bonds were issued which wealthy men were compelled to sign, *after* which the amount of money they were to pay the crown was filled in. Thus *subscribe them* (l. 50) means not writing in the names on the charters (as OED would have it), but rather (as in Ure, New Arden edition, p. 44) writing in the amount to be paid, on charters already signed. Evidently the 'loans' made for this scheme of collecting revenue were never repaid.

53 Bushy, what news So reads F (see I.4.1SD N.), while Q at this point has, instead of a speech, only the stage direction *Enter Bushie with newes*. Wilson and Sisson both take *Bushy* in this line to be an editorial addition to F and so spurious.

Act II, Scene 1

18 of whose . . . fond So reads Q except that *fond* (from J. P. Collier) has been substituted for Q's *found* (which was doubtless taken over from the last word of the next line). Q2, by printing *state* for *taste* (*of whose state the wise are found*), began a series of odd readings: *of his state: then there are found*, in other Qq; and *of his state: then there are sound*, in F. Although some editors think the sense of the words as printed here requires a negative or some other alteration (Wilson is inclined toward W. N. Lettsom's conjecture of *th' unwise* for *the wise*), they may well mean, 'like flattery, which even the wise (including Richard) have a fond taste for.'

40–55 **This royal . . . Jewry** This highly eloquent and very famous speech on patriotism was so popular as to be included (except l. 50) in *England's Parnassus* (1600), although it was then mistakenly attributed to Michael Drayton. (A phonetic transcription of the speech, ll. 40–68, is printed in Kökeritz, *Shakespeare's Pronunciation*, pp. 358–9.) The ultimate source of the speech is Froissart.

68SD **Enter . . . Willoughby** *Bushy* is Sir John Bushy, Speaker of the House of Commons; *Green* Sir Henry Green, Justice of the King's Bench (under Edward III); *Bagot* Sir William Bagot, Sheriff of Leicestershire; *Ross* William, Lord Ross, Lord Treasurer (under Henry IV); *Willoughby* William, Lord Willoughby, a Knight of the Garter. In Qq this direction appears after l. 70.

70 **rag'd** Slightly altering Joseph Ritson's reading *rein'd*, Sisson reads *raynd* (i.e. 'reined,' or 'reined in') for Q's *ragde*, to correct what seems to him a pointless aphorism.

73–83 **O, how . . . bones** Many have found Gaunt's punning ludicrously unsuited to a dying man, but Coleridge sees it otherwise: 'On a death-bed there is a feeling which may make all things appear but as puns and equivocations. And a passion there is that carries off its own excess by plays on words' (*Coleridge's Shakespearean Criticism*, ed. T. M. Raysor, 2 vols. Cambridge, Harvard University Press, 1930).

94 **Ill . . . ill** A triple meaning: 'I who see you am ill'; 'I am ill at what I see'; and 'what I see in you is ill (evil).' Usually the line is read as an alexandrine.

95–6 **Thy . . . sick** Gaunt is comparing his own actual deathbed with the *deathbed* of the *sick* (i.e. evil) king, which is as broad as the whole nation.

100–13 **A thousand . . . king** Lily B. Campbell, in *Shakespeare's 'Histories'* (San Marino, California, Huntington Library Publications, 1947), pp. 199–200, describes 'the sins which were brought up time after time when the fate of Richard II was pointed out to Elizabeth as a warning': being swayed by favorites, spilling the royal blood, and leasing out her kingdom (in the form of land grants and other special privileges).

111 **But . . . land** 'But since your possessions are limited to this one country.'

115 **And thou . . . lunatic** So read the Qq; F reads *And—/* Richard. *And thou, a lunaticke.*

126 **like the pelican** Young pelicans were fabled to feed on the heart's blood of the mother bird, just as Richard, according to Gaunt, has been draining and spilling the lifeblood of his royal family. In addition, the pelican is a Christian symbol for self-sacrifice. (See also *Hamlet*, IV.5.145–7.)

145–6 **As . . . mine** Richard is purposely twisting York's words to make them mean: 'as Bolingbroke loves me, so does Gaunt; as they both love me, so I love them'—which is to say, not at all.

168 **marriage . . . disgrace** The exiled Bolingbroke would have married the King of France's cousin had not Richard sent the Earl of Salisbury to prevent the match. The event is described in Holinshed, but the *disgrace* to which York refers is not explained there or in any other known source.

186–8 **Why . . . withal** The pentameters are indicated by the present arrangement of lines, which differs from that in Q. The reading *withal* (from Q2; Q has *with all*) means here 'with not being pardoned.'

202 **letters-patents** Open letters from the king by which certain rights were conferred. (The modern form would be 'letters patent.')

252–4 **Wars . . . blows** The allusion is to the treaty Richard first made with Charles VI of France in 1393 and renewed in 1396 when he married Isabelle. The *compromise* refers to the cession of Brest by Richard to the Duke of Brittany in 1397.

277 **Le Port Blan** Written *le Port Blan* in Qq, *Port le Blan* in F,

and *Le port blanc* in Holinshed, this is a small port in Côtes du Nord.

279–81 Cobham . . . Exeter Since Cobham had nothing to do with the Duke of Exeter, a line must be lost. Edmond Malone's edition of 1790 first supplies: 'The son of Richard, Earl of Arundel' (the *his* of l. 282 thus referring to the late earl).

284 Quoint Although Qq read *Coines*, most editors print *Quoint*, following F, which is only another spelling of Holinshed's *Coint*.

Act II, Scene 2

38 'Tis . . . possess 'That which I feel is destined to be mine later on.' It is as though the grief is someone else's property which is to come to her in the future.

89 Sirrah . . . Gloucester As printed in Qq and F, some of York's lines (like this and ll. 116 and 119) are excessively long, while others (like ll. 91 and 107) are short. It seems likely that this irregularity, as well as the actual wording of York's speech, is Shakespeare's way of suggesting the aged, unsteady, and reticent condition of his character.

89 Plashie Actually York's sister died not in Pleshy but Barking, and later than this.

132 Bristow Here Qq read *Brist.* and F reads *Bristoll*, but elsewhere (II.3.163 and III.2.142) both Qq and F read *Bristow*. Since this latter spelling indicates pronunciation it is retained throughout.

Act II, Scene 3

70 my answer . . . Lancaster 'My answer is that I answer only to the title of Lancaster'—i.e. not to Hereford.

80 self-borne So read Qq, F, but since no Elizabethan distinction was made between the spellings *borne* and *born*, some editors adopt F3's *self-born*, meaning 'home-sprung,' i.e. productive of civil strife, and relate it to *native* nearby.

106 On what . . . wherein 'On what quality or fault of mine is it based, and in what does it consist?'

113 for Lancaster Which is to say that Bolingbroke comes either 'as Lancaster' or 'to claim the title and rights of the Duke of Lancaster.'

Act III, Scene 1

43 Glendor Owen Glendower, Richard's squire and minstrel, did, historically speaking, escape to Wales but not until later. Verity and Wilson express the possibility, and Sisson the certainty, that the 'Welsh Captain' in II.4 is Glendower himself.

Act III, Scene 2

1 Barkloughly Castle There is no such place. The name, written *Barclowlie* in Holinshed, is Holinshed's mistake for Harlech (i.e. Hertlowli) Castle in Wales.

21 double Shakespeare here falls into the popular misconception that a venomous snake poisons with its tongue rather than its fangs.

29–32 The means . . . redress This troublesome passage is printed here as it appears in all the Qq (F omits it), but with Pope's addition of *if* to complete both the meaning and meter of l. 30. Most editions follow Pope's other changes in the passage as well, but this seems like challenging the authority of all the Qq unnecessarily, since their version of the lines is acceptable in every other respect.

37 eye of heaven John Gower refers to Richard as 'Sol,' and Richard's tomb in Westminster Abbey bears the sign of the sun. Furthermore sun imagery is prominent through most of the play, for description of which see Paul Reyher, 'Le symbole du soleil dans la tragédie de "Richard II,"' *Revue de l'enseignement des langues vivantes*, *40* (1923), 254–60; Caroline Spurgeon, *Shakespeare's Imagery* (New York, Macmillan, 1935); W. H. Clemen, *The Development of Shakespeare's Imagery* (London, Methuen, 1951); and Samuel Kliger, 'The Sun Imagery in *Richard II*,' *Studies in Philology*, *45* (1948), 196–202.

55 off . . . anointed By omitting *off* F normalizes the meter, but since 'noint' was a common form of 'anoint' it does as well to read *an anointed* as three syllables.

141

122 **Where is Bagot** Since l. 132 mentions *three* traitors, since Aumerle does not mention Bagot in l. 141, and since we presume (from II.2.138) that Bagot has gone to join Richard in Ireland, most editors have taken the words *Where is Bagot?* to be either a corruption of the text or a lapse of memory on Shakespeare's part. But because Richard always associates the name of Bagot with the others and knows nothing of him at this time, it might seem queer if he did *not* mention Bagot. What Shakespeare knows is, in short, not identical with what Richard knows at this point. Had he chosen to, Shakespeare might have had someone (like Aumerle) explain to Richard that Bagot tried to join him in Ireland.

134 **Make war . . . this** So Q; F prints *make warre* with l. 133 and feebly ends the line with *this Offence* (Q has *this* alone).

Act III, Scene 3

14 **For . . . head** This almost parenthetical phrase probably means 'for omitting (i.e. taking away) his title,' but may mean 'for taking such liberties,' just as we speak of a frisky horse 'taking its head.'

39 **my** Here, as in a few other places, the speech shifts to the first person singular in order to avoid confusion for the playgoers.

40–1 **Provided . . . granted** 'Provided that the repeal of my banishment and the restoration of my lands be freely granted.' Grammatically (the construction is Latin), the subject of the clause is *my banishment . . . again.*

61SD **Parle . . . Salisbury** In this direction taken from F (and slightly augmented), *Parle* refers to the trumpet call used to summon forces to parley. *On the walls* here no doubt indicates Richard's entrance on the upper stage.

93–4 **He is . . . war** 'Bolingbroke has come to open the blood-stained will of war to claim its legacy.'

103 **thrice-noble** Perhaps *thrice* is merely emphatic, although it may have a definite meaning: Bolingbroke, already Duke of Hereford and Earl of Derby, is now claiming the title of Duke of Lancaster.

119 **is a prince, is just** Q and Q2 read *is princesse iust;* other Qq

read *is a Prince iust;* F reads *is a Prince, is iust.* Though these shifting readings are a sure sign of trouble, this edition and most others follow F. A recent interpretation by Sisson in *New Readings in Shakespeare, 2,* 24, is worth considering, however. He judges the compositor to have read 'prince *e* iust' in his copy as 'princes iust' instead of 'prince and just,' by mistaking the ampersand for an *s,* and then to have set 'princes,' quite naturally, as *princesse.* But this reading is not without difficulties: we cannot be sure how Shakespeare (or a copyist) wrote ampersands; there is no available proof that Shakespeare (or the copyist) would have used the spelling 'princes' rather than 'princesse'; nor is Sisson able to complete the line using Q alone, since in the interest of meter and idiom he too must borrow the word *a* from Q3. The reading almost universally adopted from F is rougher and less idiomatic than Sisson's, but at least it is based on the revised readings of two critically reputable texts, Q3 and F.

178 **Phaëton** The son of Apollo who, because he lost control of the horses drawing the chariot of the Sun and drove so near the earth as almost to set it on fire, was hurled to the earth by a bolt of Zeus. Phaëton (knowledge of whom came chiefly from Ovid's *Metamorphoses*) was a favorite subject of Elizabethan emblem writers.

204–5 **too young . . . heir** Although Richard and Bolingbroke were both thirty-three at this time, Shakespeare consistently suggests that Richard is young and Bolingbroke middle-aged.

Act III, Scene 4

5 **bias** OED indicates three meanings for the word: the way of rolling the ball, its course, and its construction. In this last sense *bias* is the lead weight inserted in one side of a bowling ball to make it 'run' in an arc so as to go around other balls lying in the path between the bowler and the jack (small white ball) he is trying to hit.

29 **apricocks** This reading from F gives the probable pronunciation (the Q spelling *Apricokes* is not significant). Apricots were not brought to England until the 14th century—another small anachronism.

30–66 Which . . . thrown down This conversation, developing a metaphorical comparison between kingship and gardening, reflects Shakespeare's love of gardens and their imaginative suggestions (compare *The Winter's Tale*, IV.4, and *Henry V*, V.2).

54–7 They are . . . year This lineation is Capell's. The lines in Qq and F end with *are*, *king*, *trimm'd*, and *year*.

105–6 rue . . . ruth A complex pun. The plant *rue* was also called 'herb of grace,' since *rue*, meaning 'repentance,' comes through God's grace. More than that, Shakespeare is also linking *rue* and *ruth*, both as they sound alike and as *rue* meaning 'repentance' resembles *ruth* meaning 'pity.'

Act IV, Scene 1

17–19 Than . . . lords Capell's lineation, which is followed here, better preserves the pentameters than does that in Qq, F, which ends the lines with *withal* and *death*. L. 19 is an alexandrine.

25 manual seal A grim joke may be meant, turning on the reference of *manual* to a gage which is a glove (or gauntlet).

40 rapier For discussion of the rapier and other dueling matters, see Horace S. Craig, 'Dueling Scenes and Terms in Shakespeare's Plays,' *University of California Publications in English*, 9 (1940), 1–28.

52 task the earth So reads Q. Most editors interpret the phrase to mean 'charge the earth with bearing my gage too.' Chambers thinks the *task* is that of the earth serving as a field of combat; Capell sidesteps the difficulty by omitting *earth* and making *task thee* into a direct challenge to Aumerle. Still another possible meaning for the line derives from the reading in the other Qq, *take the earth:* 'I take the earth as my witness in returning the challenge to you, Aumerle.' In any case, as C. H. Herford properly observes (Warwick edition, 1893): 'the high-flown language is in keeping with the conventional tone of the challenge.'

60 Surrey Thomas Holland, third Earl of Kent, was created Duke of Surrey in 1397 and, as Richard's nephew, was naturally on Aumerle's side.

154–318 May it please . . . king's fall These celebrated lines comprising the so-called 'deposition scene' did not appear in the first three Qq of 1597, 1598, and 1598, while Queen Elizabeth was alive and sensitive to reports encouraging her own abdication. Though proof is lacking, the prevailing scholarly opinion is that the lines were written as an original part of the play, were regularly spoken on the stage, but were withheld from print for political reasons, or were actually censored. (The words *woeful pageant* in l. 321 reinforce the idea that the lines were spoken.) The passage was printed for the first time a few years after the queen's death—in Q4 (1608)—and has been printed as part of the play ever since. The present text is based on F, which in all but one or two details is superior to both Q4 and Q5 (1615). (See Appendix A.) As a matter of historical fact Richard did not appear in person before the assembled parliament to make his resignation.

238 bait The figure is from sport, in which dogs charged and baited a bull or bear which was tied to a stake. Here *wretchedness* is one of the dogs.

262 To melt . . . drops The line echoes the close of Marlowe's *Doctor Faustus:* 'O soul, be changed into little water-drops, And fall into the ocean, ne'er be found,' just as ll. 281–6 below echo the famous passage earlier in Act V of *Faustus:* 'Was this the face that launch'd a thousand ships, And burnt the topless towers of Ilium?'

276–85 Give me . . . follies This arrangement of lines follows F. Because of three omissions in Q4 and Q5 (*and . . . read* in l. 276, *Thou dost . . . me* in l. 281, and *Was . . . winke* in ll. 283–4), the line arrangement is different there.

319–20 On . . . yourselves This reading is from F. The words in Q (which J. Dover Wilson in his edition calls 'a patch designed to cover the rent in the text made by the exclusion of the "Deposition" scene') reads:

> Let it be so, and loe on wednesday next,
> We solemnly proclaime our Coronation,
> Lords be ready all.

Henry was crowned on Monday, October 13, 1399.

320 coronation 'It is significant for a study of Shakespeare's handling of history that he writes a deposition scene that is not in his sources, and omits a spectacular coronation that is' (Llewellyn M. Buell, Yale edition, 1921).

Act V, Scene 1

1 Queen This scene of parting is not historical. The final separation occurred at Windsor, as represented in II.2.1–4.

54 With . . . France The idea is not historical. Only after Bolingbroke had detained Isabelle at Sonning for several months did he allow her to return to France (in July 1401).

88 Better . . . the near Which is to say, 'it is better that we be far apart than near yet not nearer'—since they will not be allowed to be together (the second *near* is comparative) even though Isabelle were to remain in England. Note the homonymic pun on *near* and *nere* (see Kökeritz, *Shakespeare's Pronunciation*, p. 131).

Act V, Scene 2

23 theater An anachronism in 1399, since the first mention of regular London theaters is around 1575. Other anachronisms are apricots (III.4.29) and the rapier (IV.1.40).

56 seal . . . hangs A seal was stamped on the lower end of a parchment strip whose other end was attached to the document. In this case the dangling seal hung outside the doublet.

67–8 Bound . . . bound to Naturally the one to whom a debtor is *bound* would hold the bond, as in *The Merchant of Venice*. Thus Aumerle has not signed the usual bond to borrow money but has sworn to join in the conspiracy to kill the new king, which was to be disguised as a tourney on Epiphany Day, 1400. See York's query (l. 52) and Aumerle's remark (l. 55); the latter has a meaning quite unsuspected by York. Historically, the place agreed upon was not Oxford but Kingston, near Windsor.

111 his horse This odd reading in all Qq and Ff may have been influenced by Holinshed: 'The Earl of Rutland . . . took his horse.'

146

Act V, Scene 3

12 So . . . crew Since the *which* (i.e. whom) of l. 10 is the object of *support*, this line is left in the air, grammatically. It may be an afterthought.

58 serpent 'An allusion to the old fable of the man who warmed a half-frozen serpent by putting it in the bosom of his garment and was stung to death' (G. L. Kittredge's edition, 1941). Compare III.2.131, and 2 *Henry VI*, III.1.343–4.

136 I . . . heart So Qq and Ff, but there is excellent justification for transposing the two halves of the line and so preserving both rhyme and meter. Modern editors almost invariably make *With all my heart* end l. 136 and *I pardon him* begin l. 137.

Act V, Scene 4

1SD Enter . . . servant F prints the eleven lines of this scene as part of scene 3. Thus the two following scenes, which F prints as scenes 4 and 5, are printed in this and other editions as scenes 5 and 6.

Act V, Scene 5

50–8 For now . . . hours 'There are three ways in which a clock notices the progress of time; viz., by the libration of the pendulum, the index on the dial, and the striking of the hour. To these the king, in his comparison, severally alludes; his sighs corresponding to the jarring of the pendulum, which, at the same time that it watches or numbers the seconds, marks also their progress in minutes on the dial or outward watch, to which the king compares his eyes; and their want of figures is supplied by a succession of tears, or, to use an expression of Milton [*Il Penseroso*, 130], *minute-drops:* his finger, by as regularly wiping these away, performs the office of the dial-point; his clamorous groans are the sounds that tell the hour' (Samuel Henley in Variorum edition of 1785). Note also the double sense of *watch* as wakefulness and as timepiece.

147

60 Jack of the clock This mechanical figure (also called Jack-o'-th'-clock-house) was a little man in armor who struck the bell each quarter hour. Compare *Richard III*, IV.2.117.

67 royal, noble Richard's pun (also said to have been made by Queen Elizabeth) is finished in l. 68. Since a *royal* or rose noble was a gold coin worth 10*s.* and the ordinary *noble* was worth 6*s.* 8*d.*, the difference between them was ten groats (a groat being worth 4*d.*).

112 die The approximate date was February 14, 1400. Richard's death at the hands of Exton is a tradition deriving from an anonymous French source which was eventually brought to England and so to Shakespeare. This version of the death does not sort with the appearance of Richard's remains exhumed in 1873 (which showed no clear signs of violence), nor with other more reputable reports of death by starvation, such as the rebel Percies' 'Letter of Defiance.' As Steel sums it up (*Richard II*, pp. 286–7), 'the Piers Exton story, which is of late and dubious origin, may therefore be rejected in favour of some form of starvation, whether self-inflicted or not, assisted possibly by smothering.' (For Holinshed's version see Appendix B.)

Act V, Scene 6

1 latest news When the plot was discovered Bolingbroke decided against going to Oxford and remained at Windsor. The rebel *duketti* who marched there to surprise him found he had fled to London by night. After retreating to Cirencester the rebels were soon attacked, beaten, and confined to the abbey of Cirencester. A trick to assist their escape by firing houses in the neighborhood succeeded only in rousing the townsmen to retaliation. It was clear that Richard could not be allowed to live and that the resistance to Bolingbroke had lost its energy when two of the leading rebels taken after the fire, the Earls of Salisbury and Kent, were beheaded about sunset on January 7, 1400.

8 Oxford . . . Kent Since we have no record of a conspirator named Oxford, the F reading is probably more accurate historically: *The heads of Salsbury, Spencer, Blunt, and Kent*. Thus *Spencer* would be Thomas Despencer (formerly Earl of Gloucester but degraded by Henry), and *Blunt* would be Sir Thomas Blunt or *Blount* (apparently no relation to Sir Walter Blunt of *Henry IV*).

52 bier Richard was buried in a common grave at Pontefract (or Pomfret). But afterward, when the false rumor spread abroad that Richard was still alive in Scotland, King Henry had the body disinterred and carried through the main cities of the realm to London. For two days it lay in Cheapside, and for a time in St. Paul's, before being carried to King's Langley where it was secluded in an 'obscure grave,' there to stay until Henry V (who was more chivalrous than his father) moved it to the beautiful tomb in Westminster Abbey, which Richard himself had built for his first wife, Anne of Bohemia. There the unfortunate king still lies, with the epitaph by Abbot Feckenham on the stone above him, serving as a motto to his character and this play: *Fuisse felicem miserrimum*—to have been fortunate was most wretched.

APPENDIX A

Text and Date

This, the fifth of Shakespeare's history plays, tells in highly
ceremonious style the story of a king's fall—a fall which promised
dramatic satisfaction both to King Richard himself in the 1390's
and, less surprisingly, to London's playgoing public in the 1590's.
The publisher, Andrew Wise, entered 'his copy' of *Richard II*
in the Stationers' Register on August 29, 1597, and there is no
reason to doubt that he acquired the play manuscript legiti-
mately. Wise is thought to have purchased it from the Lord
Chamberlain's Men, the company of players to which Shakespeare belonged, after Shakespeare had sold the company his
rights to it. The absence of the playwright's name on the title
page strongly suggests that Shakespeare had little reputation in
1597, but as the play sold well and had, according to Wilson,
'one of the most successful runs recorded for Elizabethan times,'
his name appeared soon after, affixed to the two editions of 1598
and again to those of 1608 and 1615, which were the last before
the First Folio of 1623.[1] It is the only play by Shakespeare which
passed through three editions in less than two years.

The First Quarto of *Richard II* is classed as a 'good quarto'
(as opposed to a 'bad quarto' or corrupt text of a play). On the
basis of thorough and expert study—and the texts of very few
Shakespearean plays have received as much attention—nearly
all editors judge the First Quarto to have come from a playhouse
manuscript in Shakespeare's (or a copyist's) hand, which was
ultimately Shakespeare's own 'foul papers' or rough copy. The
evidence for this rests mainly on the First Quarto's graphic but
incomplete stage directions, its inconsistent designation of charac-

---

1. For a summary description of the Qq and F, see the *New Variorum Edition of Shakespeare: The Life and Death of King Richard the
Second*, ed. Matthew W. Black (Philadelphia, J. B. Lippincott, 1955),
pp. 355–91.

ters, and (according to some scholars) its punctuation.[2] It was, all in all, a very fine text which came from the printshop of Valentine Simmes in September of 1597 and went on sale at the Sign of the Angel, Wise's shop in Paul's Churchyard.

For reasons of political expediency, if not outright censorship, the First Quarto omits a crucial passage from the play, the so-called 'deposition scene' (IV.1.154–318). Therefore, this edition derives from a combination of the First Quarto of 1597 and, for the 'deposition scene,' the First Folio of 1623. While previous editors have almost without exception adopted this choice of texts, they have varied in the extent to which they have adhered to them. In accordance with the editorial policy for the series, the present edition makes as few departures as possible from its copy texts, fewer than are made in any other edition of the play. Only about seventy departures from the First Quarto (hereafter called Q) and four departures from the 'deposition scene' in the First Folio (called F) have been deemed important enough to call for acknowledgment in the glosses or notes, although other categorical departures occur, shortly to be noted.

Q, regarded as a comparatively rare edition, is known to exist in four copies: the Huth (in the British Museum), the Capell (in Trinity College, Cambridge), the Petworth (in Petworth Castle), and the Devonshire (in the Huntington Library). Although no one of these copies is exactly like another,[3] the differences among them are, for the most part, of little significance to the general reader. In the ten or twelve cases where the differences are important they have been noted in the glosses. Nevertheless, the text of Q as it stands is by no means free from diffi-

---

2. Among the scanty stage directions in Q are such informal and vivid ones as: *He pluckes it out of his bosome and reades it* (V.2.71) and *The murderers rush in* (V.5.104). Speech-tags in Q are not consistent: Bolingbroke appears as *Bullingbrooke*, *Herford*, and *King*; Mowbray as both *Mowbray* and *Norfolk*. Q's punctuation is careful and dramatic in the set speeches, and especially there seems to show Shakespeare's hand.

3. A brief comparison of the copies of Q appears in the *New Variorum Edition*, pp. 357–9.

culties. As Pollard observes, 'on an average one error has been discovered on every page of the First Quarto, and . . . about once in every four pages there is a word or a phrase . . . for which no satisfactory solution can be discovered.'[4] For this reason, and for the purpose of bringing the reader into closer touch with Shakespeare's words, the glosses printed at the foot of each page in this edition are particularly full. (Meanings and usages to be found in *Webster's New Collegiate Dictionary* have nearly always been eliminated, however.)

The text of *Richard II* printed here follows Q, with the exception of (1) instances cited in the glosses or notes, and (2) certain departures made to assist the modern student in hearing and understanding the verse lines without doing violence to what Shakespeare wrote. The latter are as follows: archaic spellings which indicate nothing about Elizabethan pronunciation have been abandoned; stage directions have been added or enlarged (usually after F);[5] punctuation has been increased (since Q is underpunctuated) or altered (modern equivalents to the marks and capitals used in Elizabethan printing have been sought); and some changes in lineation have been made, for which F has often served as a valuable check. As in many other editions, elision is indicated not according to the copy texts but according to what the meter requires. (See the note to I.1.63.) Also, in some recurrent instances where F is more modern or more correct than Q, F has been followed without comment: *sit* (Q *set*), *thee* (Q *the*), *thine* (Q *thy*), *mine* (Q *my*) or the reverse, *my* (Q *mine*). Finally there is the troublesome problem of pronunciation. Although pronunciation is often problematical and one word may sometimes be pronounced in different ways, the intention in this edition is to preserve all copy-text spellings which indicate pronunciation. (For the special problem of past participles and verbs in the past tense, see the note to I.2.30.) Pronunciation of proper names is no exception: wherever their spelling in the copy text

---

4. Alfred W. Pollard, *A New Shakespeare Quarto: The Tragedy of King Richard II* (London, Quaritch, 1916), pp. 33–4.

5. For the stage directions in this edition, see note to I.1.195SD.

indicates Elizabethan pronunciation (which may not be like that current today), the old forms are retained (e.g. *Bullingbrooke, Herford, Callice* for Calais, *Rainold* for Reginald). Although the spelling of unstressed syllables is not reproduced precisely as in Q, the forms of the names printed here are the forms which recur most frequently.

The particular attention given to pronunciation, lineation, and metrical values in this edition only recognizes that *Richard II*, together with *King John* and Parts 1 and 3 of *Henry VI*, is one of four Shakespearean plays written entirely in verse. Quite as much as it is a stage play, *Richard II* is a stately and stylized dramatic poem. Three-quarters of its lines are blank verse—more than in any major tragedy except *Antony and Cleopatra*—and more pentameter rhymes occur in it than in any other plays except *Love's Labour's Lost* and *A Midsummer Night's Dream*.

After Q came the Second and Third Quartos in 1598. The Second (Q2) is in most respects poor. Printed from a copy of Q unlike any of the four surviving, it introduces more errors than it corrects, whereas Q3, which derives from it, was executed with great care and may well have been the printed source of F. Q4 and Q5, the latter being only a docile copy of the former, were printed in 1608 and 1615. In Q4 for the first time the 'deposition scene' was printed, though badly.

The First Folio text of *Richard II*, issued in 1623, is a well-edited work, but the question of its origin makes it the most controversial of the *Richard* texts. F is a thorough reworking of the play which succeeds in correcting about one-third of Q's original errors, about half of the new errors in Q2 and Q3, and nearly all the new errors in Q4 and Q5. And yet the number of fresh errors it introduces shows how difficult the text of *Richard II* is, even for the very capable editors of F.

F's text of the play shows signs of having been prepared for the theater as well as the private reader. As Wilson says, it bears 'all the stigmata of prompt-book.'[6] Not only do the play-house cuts amount to fifty-one lines but the stage directions are

---

6. Wilson's New Cambridge edition, p. 111.

greatly enlarged, the punctuation is far heavier, the verse lines are made more regular, the supernumeraries in III.4 clarified, and the speech-tags normalized.

Though the best opinions on the intricate question of F's origin are still unreconciled and the majority still favor Q5, the most recent authority, W. W. Greg, moves with Pollard and Hasker toward the conclusion that Q3 was the primary textual source of F.[7] It is generally supposed that the quarto used—whichever it was—was collated with some independent authority originating in the theater. Some scholars judge the independent authority to have been a playhouse promptbook, but the matter is no more certain than the matter of whether the independent authority was printed or in manuscript. According to Greg, while the case for Q3 is 'virtually conclusive,'[9] the case for Q5 as basis for the last 151 lines of the play (which were missing from the Q3 copy used for F) is 'a strong one, if less compelling.'

The 'deposition scene' printed in F is judged by Greg and others to come from a reputable playhouse manuscript, presumably a promptbook.[10] No one doubts that F took the scene from an authentic manuscript while Q4's scene came from a very inferior copy. Furthermore, almost no one doubts that the scene was, from the beginning, presented on the stage, even though it was not printed until 1608.

7. See W. W. Greg, *The Shakespeare First Folio* (Oxford, Oxford University Press, 1955), pp. 236–8; Pollard, *A New Shakespeare Quarto*, pp. 52–3; Richard E. Hasker, 'The Copy for the First Folio *Richard II*,' *Studies in Bibliography: Papers of the Bibliographical Society of the University of Virginia*, 5 (1952–53), [53]–72.

8. See Pollard, *A New Shakespeare Quarto*, pp. 51, 89, 98–9; Hasker, 'First Folio *Richard II*,' pp. 55–8, 70; also see Greg, *The Shakespeare First Folio*, pp. 237–8; and for his theory of a two-manuscript source, Wilson's New Cambridge edition, pp. 108–14.

9. Evidence in support of Q3 as source includes: *unpruind* for *unprund* (III.4.45); *mine* for *my* (IV.1.70); 97 errors in Q3 which were retained by F. Hasker, 'First Folio *Richard II*,' pp. 62–3, finds strong support for Q3 in the punctuation of F.

10. Greg, *The Shakespeare First Folio*, pp. 236–7.

Plain and sure evidence for the dating of *Richard II* does not exist. We know that it cannot have been written later than the publication of Q in 1597 (or than the mention of the play in Meres' *Palladis Tamia* in 1598) and assume that it came somewhat earlier. Most scholars give 1597 as the approximate date, though a few, preferring not to fix it so exactly, merely include *Richard II* in the 'lyric group' of plays written between 1593 and 1596. Three kinds of 'evidence' are usually presented in support of the year 1595. The style, which is characteristically early and is similar to that of *Romeo and Juliet* and *King John*, shows such features as: a large number of rhymes (one-fifth of the play's 2,728 lines), quatrains in three places, and a strong inclination toward end-stopped lines. The other kinds of 'evidence' are: (1) passages in Daniel's *Civil Wars* (1595) believed to resemble parts of *Richard II* (see Appendix B), and (2) a contemporary letter from Sir Edward Hoby to Sir Robert Cecil which mentions a performance of a play called *Richard II* in 1595. Although there are scholars who deny that Daniel is relevant or that Hoby's letter refers to a *Richard II* recently written by Shakespeare, the opinion of those willing to use these three arguments as evidence points, if inexactly, to 1595 as the date of composition.[11]

By now it is generally assumed that *Richard II* was first played during the fall season of 1595. Someone, perhaps Essex who very early took a fancy to the play, soon saw in it an application to current political affairs,[12] a consideration which led to the suppression of the 'deposition scene' during Queen Elizabeth's lifetime. But the exclusion of that climactic scene did not prevent the play from being performed. Even if Elizabeth, in her pique, was using the word 'forty' only as a round figure, she is said to have remarked, 'This tragedy was played forty times in open

11. See both Sir Edmund Chambers, 'The Date of Richard II,' *Review of English Studies*, 1 (1925), 75–6, and a summary of the evidence in the *New Variorum Edition*, pp. 393–5.

12. See Wilson's New Cambridge edition, pp. xvi–xxxiv, and Ure's New Arden edition, pp. lvii–lxii. (I have been unable to find the Papal Bull many editors refer to as having been issued in 1596 to stir Elizabeth's subjects against her and so depose her.)

streets and houses.' We next hear of *Richard II* being presented, and for reasons now rather obscure, on the eve of the Essex Rebellion, February 24, 1601. Other performances occurred later on, like that recorded for 1607 on board the 'Dragon,' a vessel lying off Sierra Leone on its way to the East Indies. The more recent record of the play shows fifty major productions since 1900. The number of performances in that time has been enormous, including those by Maurice Evans who played the role of Richard about four hundred times between 1937 and 1940.[13]

Richard II has been studied by an incomparable group of Shakespearean scholars, and to them, as well as to the general editors of the present series, I owe a great debt of gratitude. All the important texts of the play have been thoroughly examined by one or another textual specialist—W. W. Greg, Richard E. Hasker, C. J. Sisson, and above all by A. W. Pollard in his exemplary introduction to Q3 published in 1916. Among the outstanding editions are those by Sir Edmund Chambers, C. H. Herford, A. W. Verity, Sir Henry Newbolt, and more recently G. B. Harrison, G. L. Kittredge, J. Dover Wilson, and Peter Ure, of which I would single out for their particular excellence those of Chambers, Verity, and Wilson. And for its countless useful features, one welcomes the recent *New Variorum Edition* produced by Matthew W. Black.

---

13. See Harold Child's account of the stage history (in Wilson's New Cambridge edition, pp. lxxvii–xcii), and Matthew W. Black's in the *New Variorum Edition*, pp. 564–75.

14. Edmund K. Chambers' Falcon edition, London, Longmans, Green, 1895; C. H. Herford's Warwick Shakespeare, London, Blackie and Son, [1863]; A. W. Verity's Pitt Press Shakespeare, Cambridge, Cambridge University Press, 1899; Henry Newbolt's edition, Oxford, Clarendon Press, 1912; G. B. Harrison's *Shakespeare: Major Plays*, New York, Harcourt, Brace, 1948; George Lyman Kittredge's edition, Boston, Ginn & Co., 1941; J. Dover Wilson's New Cambridge edition, Cambridge, Cambridge University Press, 1939; and Peter Ure's New Arden edition, Cambridge, Harvard University Press, 1956.

APPENDIX B

Sources

While no one denies the truth of Wilson's statement that 'Holinshed furnishes the plain hempen warp upon which the colourful historical tapestry we call *Richard II* was woven,'[1] the other threads of the fabric have been endlessly woven and unwoven. Shakespeare's principal source for the play is the second edition (1587) of Raphael Holinshed's *Chronicles of England, Scotland, and Ireland*, and in addition eight other sources have been proposed, with more or less probability: five other chronicles, a verse history, and two early plays (one of them hypothetical). Before we turn to Holinshed it may be well to look briefly at these possible sources, remembering that new evidence might come along to buoy up the cases for some of them and sink others.

1. The 'Old Play.' The case for a hypothetical play, first presented in the 19th century and urged more recently by Chambers, Wilson, and Feuillerat (very emphatically by the latter two), has been carefully argued despite the lack of any proof for its existence. The play may well have existed, but until its exact nature is known and the many descriptions of it become one, the 'Old Play' shall continue to befog the issue of sources.[2]

2. Edward Hall, *The Union of the Two Noble and Illustrate Famelies of Lancastre & Yorke* (1548). Hall, the predecessor upon whom Holinshed chiefly depended for his Richard material, and occasionally even for his wording, is generally regarded as Shakespeare's direct source only in scenes 2 and 3 of the last act. These scenes, concerning Aumerle's complicity in the plot against Bolingbroke, bear close resemblance to both sources. (See Holinshed below, passage *b*.) Wilson believes the germ of another passage, Richard's famous abdication speech (III.3.143–59), to have come from Hall.[3]

1. New Cambridge edition, pp. li–lii.
2. See Wilson's New Cambridge edition, pp. lxiv–lxxv.
3. See p. 12 of the 1809 edition.

3. French sources. (a) 'Créton' or John Webb's *Translation of a French Metrical History of the Deposition of King Richard* (1399). (b) '*Traïson*' or *Chronicque de la Traïson et Mort de Richart Deux Roy Dengleterre* (?1412). (c) 'Jean Le Beau' or *La Chronique de Richard II* (between 1399 and 1449).[4] The use to which Shakespeare may have put these works, as well as their interrelation, are matters still very imperfectly understood, although some scholars consider 'Créton' and *Traïson* to be the same account, and 'Le Beau' to be a version of *Traïson*. In the opinions of Paul Reyher and Wilson, Shakespeare consulted all three (see, e.g., the description of Gloucester's death by beheading, I.1.101–3 N, which is unique to 'Le Beau'). Wilson believes the chief debt of Shakespeare to 'Le Beau' or *Traïson* to be in the conception of Richard's character after his downfall.[5]

4. 'Woodstock' or *The First Part of the Reign of King Richard the Second or Thomas of Woodstock* (c. 1591; Malone Society Reprints, 1929). Thorough and repeated study of this anonymous play reveals a large number of verbal parallels to Shakespeare's play. The prevailing opinion among scholars who assume that *Thomas of Woodstock* preceded Shakespeare's play is that Shakespeare knew it quite well and very frequently echoes its wording in the first two acts of *Richard II* (although Feuillerat is doubtful that Shakespeare ever read it). Some scholars judge the characterization of Gloucester as a 'plain well-meaning soul' to derive from *Thomas of Woodstock*, contrasting as it does with the unfavorable picture presented by Holinshed, Froissart, and Daniel.

5. Samuel Daniel, *The First Fowre Bookes of the Civile Wars Between the Two Houses of Lancaster and Yorke* (1595). The first two books of Daniel's work show constant and very close correspondence with Shakespeare's play, although indebtedness has not been proved finally. (Feuillerat believes that Shakespeare

---

4. This is printed in Buchon's *Collection des Chroniques Nationales Françaises*, vol. 15, supplement 2, p. 10.

5. See Wilson's whole argument, New Cambridge edition, pp. lviii–lxi, 211.

need not have known Daniel and that resemblances between them
originate in the hypothetical 'Old Play.') The prevailing opinion
now, however, moves toward the belief that Shakespeare was
reading the poem as he composed. Daniel's influence has been
felt in numerous passages,[6] among them V.4, where Exton ex-
plains the source of his murder motive.

6. *The Third and Fourthe Boke of Syr Johan Froissart of the
Chronycles of Englande . . . Translated . . . By Johan Bourchier
. . . Lorde Berners* (1525). Recent scholars, beginning with Reyher, believe that Shakespeare's debt to Froissart is far greater
than was suspected earlier. The most important contribution
made by Froissart, according to Wilson, is in the characterization
of John of Gaunt, especially Gaunt's attitude toward Richard,
his deathbed scene, and his famous 'Methinks I am a prophet
new inspir'd' as well as later speeches.[7]

7. Holinshed's *Chronicles*. None of Shakespeare's history plays,
including *Henry V*, stays closer to Holinshed. The main departures from Holinshed's content are alterations in time, place,
and characterization. Additions to Holinshed are, however, numerous: the conversation between Gaunt and the Duchess of
Gloucester (I.2), Gaunt's deathbed scene (II.1), the meeting of
Northumberland, Ross, and Willoughby (II.1), the appearances
of the queen (especially II.2, III.4, V.1), Richard's presence in
the deposition scene (IV.1), the Duchess of York's defense of
Aumerle (V.2 and 3), and Exton's appearance with Richard's
coffin (V.6). Also Richard's soliloquies were written independently
of Holinshed and all other sources.

To understand the relationship between Shakespeare's play
and its main source, one should read continuously that part of
Holinshed's third volume covering the late years of Richard's
reign (in the 1587 edition, pp. 486–519; in the Boswell-Stone
edition, pp. 77–130). Here follow three passages from Holinshed,

---

6. See Llewellyn M. Buell's Yale edition, pp. 126–7, and Wilson's
New Cambridge edition, pp. xl–xliv, 156–7, 205, 235.

7. See Wilson's New Cambridge edition, pp. xliv–xlv, liv–lvii,
140, 199–200.

with the corresponding parts of Shakespeare's play in each case noted. For ease of comparison, the spelling and punctuation of the passages have been modernized.

a. The death of Gaunt (compare II.1.148–214): 'The death of this duke gave occasion of increasing more hatred in the people of this realm toward the King; for he seized into his hands all the goods that belonged to him, and also received all the rents and revenues of his lands, which ought to have descended unto the Duke of Hereford by lawful inheritance, in revoking his letters-patent which he had granted to him before, by virtue whereof he might make his attorneys-general to sue livery for him of any manner of inheritances or possessions that might from thenceforth fall unto him, and that his homage might be respited, with making reasonable fine: whereby it was evident that the King meant his utter undoing.

'This hard dealing was much misliked of all the nobility, and cried out against of the meaner sort. But, namely, the Duke of York was therefore sore moved, who before this time had borne things with so patient a mind as he could, though the same touched him very near, as the death of his brother the Duke of Gloucester, the banishment of his nephew the said Duke of Hereford, and other more injuries in great number, which, for the slippery youth of the King, he passed over for the time, and did forget as well as he might.'

b. The conspiracy against Bolingbroke (compare V.2.52–117 and V.3.23–146): 'At length, by the advice of the Earl of Huntington, it was devised that they should take upon them a solemn joust, to be enterprised between him and twenty on his part, and the Earl of Salisbury and twenty with him, at Oxford, to the which triumph King Henry should be desired; and when he should be most busily regarding the martial pastime, he suddenly should be slain and destroyed, and so by that means King Richard, who as yet lived, might be restored to liberty, and have his former estate and dignity. . . . This Earl of Rutland, departing before from Westminster to see his father, the Duke of York, as he sat at dinner had his counterpane [copy] of the indenture of the confederacy in his bosom.

'The father, espying it, would needs see what it was; and

though the son humbly denied to show it, the father being more earnest to see it, by force took it out of his bosom, and perceiving the contents thereof, in a great rage caused his horses to be saddled out of hand and . . . incontinently mounted on horseback, to ride toward Windsor to the King, to declare to him the malicious intent of [his son and] his accomplices.

'The Earl of Rutland, seeing in what danger he stood, took his horse and rode another way to Windsor, in post, so that he got thither before his father; and when he was alighted at the castle gate, he caused the gates to be shut, saying that he must needs deliver the keys to the King. When he came before the King's presence, he kneeled down on his knees, beseeching him of mercy and forgiveness, and declaring the whole matter unto him in order as everything had passed, obtained pardon. Therewith came his father, and, being let in, delivered the indenture which he had taken from his son unto the King, who thereby perceiving his son's words to be true, changed his purpose for his going to Oxford.'

   c. *The death of King Richard* (compare V.4 and V.5.95–118): 'Our writer, which seemeth to have great knowledge of King Richard's doings, saith that King Henry, sitting on a day at his table, sore sighing, said, "Have I no faithful friend which will deliver me of him whose life will be my death, and whose death will be the preservation of my life?" This saying was much noted of them which were present, and especially of one called Sir Piers of Exton. This knight incontinently departed from the court, with eight strong persons in his company, and came to Pomfret, commanding the esquire that was accustomed to sew and take the assay before King Richard, to do so no more, saying, "Let him eat now, for he shall not long eat." King Richard sat down to dinner, and was served without courtesy or assay, whereupon, much marveling at the sudden change, he demanded of the esquire why he did not his duty: "Sir (he said), I am otherwise commanded by Sir Piers of Exton, which is newly come from King Henry." When King Richard heard that word, he took the carving-knife in his hand, and struck the esquire on the head, saying, "The devil take Henry of Lancaster and you together!" And with that word Sir Piers entered the chamber, well armed, with eight tall men likewise armed, every of them having a bill in his hand.

'King Richard, perceiving this, put the table from him, and stepping to the foremost man, wrung the bill out of his hands, and so valiantly defended himself that he slew four of those that thus came to assail him. Sir Piers being half dismayed herewith, leapt into the chair where King Richard was wont to sit, while the other four persons fought with him, and chased him about the chamber. And in conclusion, as King Richard traversed his ground from one side of the chamber to another, and coming by the chair where Sir Piers stood, he was felled with a stroke of a pole-axe which Sir Piers gave him upon the head, and therewith rid him out of life, without giving him respite once to call to God for mercy of his passed offences.'

In contrast to Wilson's view of Shakespeare's extreme indebtedness to his sources, see the sanely sceptical views of Peter Ure and Matthew W. Black.[8] The most comprehensive exposition of Shakespeare's possible sources is to be found in Black's *New Variorum Edition.*[9]

8. Ure's New Arden edition, pp. xxx–l, and Black's 'The Sources of Shakespeare's *Richard II*,' in *Joseph Quincy Adams Memorial Studies* (Washington, 1948), pp. 199–216.

9. Pp. 405–505.

APPENDIX C

Reading List

RICHARD D. ALTICK, 'Symphonic Imagery in *Richard II*,' *PMLA*, *62* (1947), 339–65.

TRAVIS BOGARD, 'Shakespeare's Second Richard,' *PMLA*, *70* (1955), 192–209.

LILY B. CAMPBELL, *Shakespeare's 'Histories*,' San Marino, 1947.

Coleridge's Shakespearean Criticism, ed., T. M. Raysor, 2 vols., Cambridge, Mass., 1930.

PAUL A. JORGENSEN, 'Vertical Patterns in *Richard II*,' *The Shakespeare Association Bulletin*, *23* (1948), 119–34.

G. WILSON KNIGHT, *The Imperial Theme*, London, 1931; 3d ed., 1951.

HELGE KÖKERITZ, *Shakespeare's Pronunciation*, New Haven, 1953.

JOHN PALMER, *Political Characters of Shakespeare*, London, 1945.

DONALD A. STAUFFER, *Shakespeare's World of Images*, New York, 1949.

ANTHONY STEEL, *Richard II*, Cambridge, England, 1941.

E. M. W. TILLYARD, *Shakespeare's History Plays*, London, 1951.

MARK VAN DOREN, *Shakespeare*, New York, 1939.